ALIGNMENT FOR ASSIGNMENT

ALSO BY WYNNE GOSS

———————————

Don't Kick the Donkey ... Ride It!

'Don't Kick The Donkey ... Ride it!', Wynne's first book, reveals how the hand of God is forever involved in the processes that turn negative situations into ones that conform you to His likeness, allowing you to see everything through His perspective, enabling you to overcome the obstacles and mountains of adversity, to achieve His destiny for your life.
You will clearly find 'letting go of everything you have ever known, to lay hold of everything you have ever dreamed of,' is not just a chapter title, but a way of life being offered to the reader.

ALIGNMENT FOR ASSIGNMENT

---

*Doorkeepers of
God's Treasury*

WYNNE GOSS D.div

ISBN: 978-0-9567277-1-8

Published by inHOPE Publishing

Cover Design by Jason A. Gatlin
http://www.jasongatlin.com

Interior Design Layout by Christopher Ballew
@chris_ballew

THANKS

I am so grateful to Jesus for the many individuals that He has used and still uses, to impact and shape my life. Some alive, some having been promoted to Heaven ahead of us. Each has deposited a portion of His eternal treasure into my heart, transforming and inspiring me to be a man, husband, father, friend and leader.

None have helped me more, or mean more to me, than my wife, my children and my grandchildren. I could never be who I am, or do all that I do, without them. I carry them in my heart every step of my journey, every second of every day. They are always on my mind. I am honored to have them all in my life and humbled that they feel the same way about me being part of theirs. It is the love I have for them that fills my heart and is one of the greatest motivations for me to fulfill the call of Jesus on my life. I would give anything and everything to make sure they are safe and protected.

If this is how I feel about my family, then how does our heavenly Father feel about His. I know He loves people so much more than I ever could. His value on every person is revealed at Calvary - they are priceless, worth every drop of the blood of His own Son. We meant so much to Him, that it became the motivation of Jesus to give His last breath to reach, rescue and restore every one of us.

Gwenda, I know the endless months of traveling, innumerable locations, beds, events and being away from our family is not easy for you. Yet, you do it all with such love and devotion, making me laugh through it all. Thank you for loving me, taking care of me, fulfilling the commission of Jesus with me and for simply doing life with me. You bring the best out of me every day. You are 'Jesus with skin on!' I love you.

I also wish to thank those of my spiritual family, who urge me on, to fulfill the assignment of God for my life. They are those, mostly unknown and unseen, from around the world, who constantly lift my hands through their prayers and words of encouragement. Their accounts of how God uses us to influence and help them through their journey in life, has been one of the most beautiful aspects of our daily walk with God. They took the time to share it with us, not realizing it would encourage us as much as themselves and become the fuel in our spiritual tank, to keep us believing we are hearing from God, understanding that what we do actually matters and helps others and it keeps us moving ever onwards. Keep them coming family!

Finally, I dedicate and commit this book into the hands of the Spirit of God, to use it as He pleases. Although somewhat controversial in it's content, may He use it to liberate and unleash His greatest weapon - the Church of Jesus Christ, to rise from her slumber, shake off all earthly restraints, stand in His assigned place and be all He intended her to be. The very portal of God's Kingdom into His creation.

Wynne Goss

CONTENTS

Forward

Endorsements

Chapter 1 . . . . The Master Key 21

Chapter 2 . . . . The Mess 33

Chapter 3 . . . . The Metamorphosis 45

Chapter 4 . . . . The Mission 57

Chapter 5 . . . . The Moment 69

Chapter 6 . . . . The Messenger 87

Chapter 7 . . . . The Message 103

Chapter 8 . . . . The Motivation 121

Chapter 9 . . . . The Method 133

Chapter 10 . . . . The Model 147

Chapter 11 . . . . The Multiplication 161

Chapter 12 . . . . The Multitude 177

Chapter 13 . . . . The Vision of *in*HOPE 191

Connect With Us

FORWARD

Luke 17:20 - 21 says;

> *"Now when He (Jesus) was asked by the Pharisees when the kingdom of God would come, He answered them and said, " The kingdom of God does not come with observation; nor will they say, ' See here! ' or ' See there! ' For indeed, the kingdom of God is within you."*

This has always been one of my favorite verses of the Bible as long as I can remember. I have always known, since being filled with the Holy Spirit of God at age 12, that there was someone much greater living inside of me. I knew that I couldn't contain Him, control Him or hush Him up, but could only allow Him to be who He is and go with Him wherever He went.

I learned early on that my steps are ordered by God my Heavenly Father and I would have to learn to walk with Him and not apart from Him. To walk with Him means that we're not always going in the direction of what is popular among men, but I am always confident that if I stay with Him, He will bring His purpose for that moment of time to fruition and I will know my responsibility in it.

God is moving in the earth through His people and He will not be stopped! He is rising up within each Believer who has said 'yes' to Him when they said 'yes' to salvation through Jesus Christ. God is concerned about His Kingdom being alive and flourishing in our individual lives, homes, communities, cities, states and nations around the world. Every believer in Christ has the same great one, Jesus, living inside of them and He wants to live through us. The Bible says that the whole earth is filled with the glory of God;

"And one cried to another "Holy, holy, holy is the Lord of hosts, the whole earth is full of His glory!" (Isaiah 6:3)

"For the earth will be filled with the knowledge of the glory of the Lord, as the waters cover the sea." (Habbakkuk 2:14)

"Then the Lord said: "I have pardoned, according to your word; but truly, as I live, all the earth shall be filled with the glory of the Lord." (Numbers 14:20 - 21)

His glory is filling the earth even as you are reading this book. You say "how could this be so?" And I say because of the Kingdom of God living inside of YOU! Yes YOU! His name is Jesus and He IS the Glory of God. Look at these verses in Hebrews Chapter 1:1 - 4;

"God, who at various times and in various ways spoke in time past to the fathers by the prophets, has in these last days spoken to us by His Son, whom He has appointed heir of all things, through whom also He made the worlds; who being the brightness of His glory and the express image of His person, and upholding all things by the word of His power, when He had by Himself purged our sins, sat down at the right hand of the Majesty on high, having become so much better than the angels, as He has by inheritance obtained a more excellent name than they."

If we look with eyes of flesh, covering the earth with the Glory of God looks impossible because our vision is limited to our own ability. But if we allow ourselves to look with the eyes of God's Spirit, we will see only possibility because everything we see requires God's authority and power to accomplish His desire. He has placed inside each of us the ability, through Him, to live a life of unlimited Supernatural, as opposed to our limited natural. His SUPER will overtake our natural.

He desires for us to prosper in all things and be in health to the same measure that our soul prospers (3 John 1:2).

I know all of this sounds almost too wonderful to be true. But it is true. If we align our spirit with the Spirit of God, everything in our life becomes realigned to live and prosper according to His Word and His desire for us. He has created us to live in a perfect environment that HE controls. Our alignment must happen from within our spirit first, then our natural will align. Father God is bringing everything into His order and man (flesh) is not able to stop it. This is God's mercy being poured out on us. Our prayers for deliverance and recovery in our personal lives and nations are being answered on God's terms, as only He knows all that is required to turn the hearts of His people back to Him.

In 2008 Holy Spirit dropped into my spirit a message to tell His people to stop going to church. At first I chuckled (out of nervousness) but very quickly understood what He was saying. He said tell My people to stop going TO church and start BEING THE Church (align with WHO I am). I understood fully what He was saying because I have a relationship with WHO lives inside of me. I am aligned to the Spirit of God. God's completed work of salvation and resurrection, His total Kingdom, inside of me! I know that Jesus' greatest desire for all of us is that we allow Him to live in and through us all the time.

As I have lived through five decades of church life and traveled full time in ministry for the last 18 years, I have come to recognize that the corporate organized system we call church has tried to align God's people from the outward hoping that will "fix" the inward. As a whole, the church has failed to be the answer to overcome the realities of life in this earth. God's people have suffered needless pain, disease, discouragement, disappointment and weariness, all because of trying to follow a systematic way of praising, praying, fellowshipping and receiving the Word of God. Too many are casualties of the war between what God is calling them to and what the religious order of church has told them they must do. If God's design for our life was to obey man and live up to man's expectations and rules, then he WOULD NOT have placed a HOLY KINGDOM inside of us!

We are accountable to God and His Word. God's design is that we all live in the abundance of His love mercy and grace in all things in our life, as Jesus did when he walked the earth in the flesh. God is more concerned about our relationship with Him and our alignment to Him rather than man and religious ways. In fact if we are completely honest, our aligning with religious ways has brought much hurt to individuals and divided the family of God to such a detrimental degree that many wounded believers and the majority of unbelievers turn away from anything that says church.

I met Wynne and Gwenda Goss in April of 2011 and my life has not been the same. They live the Kingdom life and never settle for anything less than what God has promised in His Word. Because they live what the preach, you will walk away from spending time with them feeling empowered and knowing your faith has increased. Wynne is my spiritual father and a true apostle in the Kingdom of God who is concerned about Jesus and His ministry being recognized among the people. He understands that it is Christ who lives in Him and it is by the Spirit of God that he lives and moves. You will always find Wynne with the people, touchable and personal. He doesn't require a platform to perform, just people to pour out the love of Jesus on.

I thank God for Wynne and his obedience to write this book. I think it is the most timely writing of our day as we need this truth NOW! This book explains the depth of God's love for us and brings into perspective the times that we are indeed living in and the critical condition of the Church. Alignment For Assignment (AFA) exposes and dismantles the religious spirit hierarchy that has infiltrated the global church and shows God's blueprint for HIS design of the Church that He is raising up. AFA disassembles and exposes all of the religious weapons that have been used against the Body of Christ. It challenges God's people as their understanding of the truth from the Word of God is exposed and brought forth. Wynne has taken the time to write the vision of our Heavenly Father and make it plain so that we can read it and RUN with it!

You may experience a stretching in your mind, soul and heart as alignment takes place in your spirit. If you believe in Jesus Christ and He is your savior then you are part of the Body of Christ and everything in and around you is shifting. The shifting is happening because Jesus is rising up on the inside of you and coming forth! God has allowed this book to fall into your hands for His purpose, it is no mistake or accident that you are reading it. I pray that you will open your spirit to receive the truth that is brought from the Word of God and your mind will be at peace to receive what God would say to you. I pray that Holy Spirit will minister to your heart love and joy as you allow a new thing to spring forth in you. You are God's chosen for such days as these and His Glory will emerge from you as you move into His alignment for your assignment.

Sandi Glee Ballew, Co-founder
Stonethrowers Ministries, Texas, USA.

ENDORSEMENTS

I've known Wynne for almost 20 years now and I know his heart well. Over the years, I've heard him preach portions of this book in different places to all kinds of people. Well now it's fully laid out at the banquet table and the feast is on! However, this is not just another book, it's Wynne's life message - his gift to the Church in which he has walked as a husband, father, pastor, leader and, most importantly, as a Christ One. This is a bold book and it will definitely challenge you as it did me. Nevertheless, I urge you to work through the tough questions to get to the crux of the matter. Allow the Holy Spirit to work His message into your heart - that the world needs to be aligned to Jesus first, not the church, because this is the genius of God's perfect order. As Wynne says, "The Church isn't meant to be built upon or around anyone, other than Jesus Christ".

Everywhere I go these days, I hear about a reformation for the church as we know it. A re-forming back to the roots of discipleship and back to the kind of church we see in Acts 2. And I, for one, am so excited by that!

Iain Williams, Campus Leader
Edge Church International, Bristol, UK.

What an amazing, challenging and transforming read. Alignment for Assignment is more than an encouraging christian resource, it's loaded with reformation principals to align the church from the organization it's become to the body it was created to be. Having clearly outlined the new creation in Christ, revelation abounds for the created function of the church. The book will no doubt leave you challenged as truth unlocks a greater awareness of the Kingdom treasure within its many members. Upon completion of the book, we could not agree more, that this book is not just some informational read, but rather an assignment flowing through Wynne's life. It's filled with His purpose and apostolic function which he wholeheartedly pours out to the body. Hidden within every chapter are nuggets of truth that reveals preparation, vision and function that has come from his alignment for assignment which is truly God's gift to the body.

Donnie & Shannon Murray, Pastors
Promise Land Church, New Orleans

Jesus said we would know the truth and the truth would set us free (John 8:31).
The truth is the Word of God, not religious traditions.
In this new book "Alignment for Assignment", Wynne takes the reader on a journey to reveal the real Truth of the Word. So much of what we call "church" is religion. I believe this book exposes the true from the false. It is so timely when so many are "done" with church meetings, but are hungry for the Kingdom of God and the Lord's presence.
It is time for all of God's family (the Church) to arise and to truly be built on the foundation of the apostles and prophets, with the cornerstone Christ Jesus Himself (Ephesians 2:20-21).

I believe every Christian needs to read this book and see just what Jesus designed Church really to be. You will be challenged, empowered and equipped. I cannot endorse this book highly enough!

Sarah Watkins
Healing 2 The Nations, Lymm, UK

I have known Wynne for almost 30 years as a true friend and faithful minister. In that time I have seen him come through good times and bad with faith, integrity and character - always representing Jesus well. Paul instructs Timothy that the best thing is to be an example to others and, for me, Wynne has remained a constant example of a good husband and father, and a true christian and minister of Christ.
Wynne carries a powerful and vital revelation, anointing and message to build the church which Jesus seeks in these days, preparing the bride for His return and aligning us as christians for the awesome assignment we still have on the earth.

Chris Horwood
Mission Siberia, UK

I believe Wynne Goss is a mighty prophetic voice for God in this day and time. The truth contained in these pages is the key to seeing revival come into your life and the world around you.

Dr. Robert Richarz, Pastor
Living Waters Church, Utopia, Texas, USA

For anyone who has ever asked themselves 'isn't there more to life than what I'm experiencing?' Or, perhaps if you have children and they ask you the repeated question on every extended road journey, 'Dad are we there yet?' 'Dad why aren't we there yet?' I highly recommend this amazing book which I believe each chapter will unlock so many doors and answer so many heart questions about your assignment and will transform the way you navigate your destiny.
I think this book is a masterpiece and I'm honored too endorse it.

Erik West - Pastor
Grace Life Church, Jemison, AL.

CHAPTER 1

The Master Key

The Key To Everything For Everyone

When the **MESSENGER** and **MESSAGE** match the **MISSION**, to restore the **MESS** in the chosen **MULTITUDE**, using God's eternal **METHOD**, **MODEL** and **MOTIVATION**, delivered at the **MOMENT** of His prompting, it brings supernatural **MULTIPLICATION** and the realignment of all things, into His likeness.

Having carried two suitcases and a guitar, up three flights of stairs in a hotel, is not the time you really want to discover your electronic room key is not working. You are faced with the dilemma of having to carry all your luggage back down the stairs, or leave them unattended outside the door, whilst you make the journey back to the reception desk in the hotel lobby. Repeatedly, I have had to pick up my luggage and descend the stairs complaining every step of the way because you know deep inside you are about to re-climb them all again, with the thought in mind, you could make this journey again only to find the key not working a second time. If you are smiling as you read this, then I guess you have been there and done it and know what I mean.

On one such occasion my head dropped at the thought of once again taking this unwanted journey, only to hear a sound at the end of the corridor that attracted my attention. I looked up. There in the distance was a maid cleaning a room. I approached her, explained my dilemma asking if she could either go and fetch me a new key, or keep an eye on my luggage whilst I did so. She beamed a beautiful smile at me and made my moment by saying, 'Sir, I have a master key that will open every door in the hotel.' She calmly walked back to my room and preceded to open my door. What I couldn't open, she could, because she had a 'master key.'

Being a preacher, I instantly saw the hidden Message in my Moment that was the Method for me to fulfill the Mission of entering my room. I was in a Mess, but a solution existed right there at that Moment in my life. It was The Master Key, known in old english as 'The Master's Key'.

I have always desired to preach messages that encourage people. But my deeper motivation has always been to share strategic insights, that act like a key that opens up the Word of God for people's lives, for the rest of their lives. I pray, that as you read the message within 'Alignment For Assignment,' it will be like someone has given you the Master Key that opens every 'door' of your life, to allow you to grow, mature and accomplish the mission the Father created you for.

The Lost Key

Adam and Eve walked with God in the Garden. It was called 'Eden' which means 'home.' They were in God's 'home' and dwelling place. They were family, not guests, therefore enjoying all the benefits of what that conveys. Every home has a culture and disciplines that keep that culture in it's place. God's home is no different. The moment Adam and Eve violated that principle He put them outside the home, closed the door behind them, placing guardian angels with flaming swords at it's entrance, to prevent them re-entering His home in a sinful condition (Gen 3:23-24). This door would remain closed to mankind until the Son of God, the Perfect Passover Lamb of God, was offered at Calvary. His blood would be sprinkled on the lintel and posts of God's eternal dwelling place, just like the very first Passover revealed (Ex 12:7). At the moment of the last breath of Jesus, the Father leaned over the balcony of Heaven and tore the veil in the Temple that kept people out of His dwelling place. The door closed for some four thousand years, had been unlocked and swung wide open because of the blood.

From that very first day when the Father put Adam and Eve outside the door, until the day of Calvary, the whole Bible records glimpses of man's knowledge of a key that opens the door back into God's home and dwelling place. The moment Adam is evicted from the garden, it reveals his family understood that an altar and an offering were the key and the door (Gen 4:3-5). The Tabernacles of Moses, David and the Temples throughout Israel's history, reveal the Lord was instructing His people to see that true worship and a perfect offering were the door and the key to His presence, power and provision.
The Old Testament also reveals that no matter how many times Israel offered the blood of lambs and bulls, or celebrated their feasts and rituals, the eternal door remained firmly shut. It would take One who's blood was perfect and innocent, who was both the Door and the blood offering, to do it on man's behalf. It was He who would be

the Key that would come and open the door on our behalf. Jesus, the Master, was both the Door and the Key (Jn 10:7-9).

Every person, ever born, has tried to find the 'key' to life. Mankind has looked for this 'key' in wealth, power, status, possessions, sex, drugs, alcohol and religion. None of them have opened the door to what they are truly looking for - peace with God and themselves. The key is not a 'thing.' It is the same person who has always been the key that makes creation work properly. It is Jesus Christ and no one and nothing else.

Ancient keys discovered by archeologists where made of shaped wood, with twine wrapped around it, with nails tapped into the wood in strategic places. The key would be placed into the lock of a door and the nails slotted into holes that matched their alignment. When the key was turned the nails would shift the bolt, or lift the latch,

---

"When Jesus came, the Messenger was the Message."

---

therefore opening the door. The key is a picture of the cross. Jesus is the Door, the cross the key into eternity's provision and abundance, for everyone who believes (John 1:12; John 10:9).

The key is more than a sermon about the cross, or the blood of Jesus. The door more than a prayer of salvation. They are a person called the Last, the First, the Beginning and the End, the Lord of Lords and King of Kings. Demons did not flee because Jesus preached a great sermon on deliverance. They fled because the One who is complete freedom and liberty was in their presence and the life of liberty within Him propelled them out of His vicinity. Lazarus rose from the dead because Life in all His fullness stood close by and called His name. Death could not contain him in the grave, because the One who is the Resurrection and the Life spoke. The sound of His voice was more than just the Galilean accent, or the grammatical way Jesus spoke. The sound of His voice carried His nature and character. Death and demons obeyed Him because of who He was, not because He preached so eloquently.

The written Word of God is powerful. The Old Testament is full of the miraculous accounts when God's Word gave His people victory, deliverance and provision. But when Jesus stepped into the earth, He had arrived with the purpose to show the Word of God in flesh is even more powerful. Jesus Christ was and is the complete revelation of the nature, character and will of God in it's entirety. He clearly stated if you want to see the Father, then look at Me (John 14:8-9). The Word in the flesh is an even greater revelation of God than the written or spoken Word. The Father didn't just send a Messenger with a Message. When Jesus came, the Messenger was the Message. They were one and the same. He lived it for all to see. He was the written Word living and breathing in the very midst of the people.

The Living Message

It is imperative every believer and follower of Jesus embrace this truth. The Spirit of God has not been given to us to help us just preach better, or do miracles to confirm our message is the real truth. He dwells within us to conform us to the likeness of Christ, that our lives become an illustrative sermon, which goes further than telling people what God is like. When what I preach is who I am, the impact is greater. If Jesus had just preached about the Father's love, without ever being the tangible expression of that love in action, then I don't believe He would have had the impact upon every generation that we see throughout history. He preached about picking up the cross and dying daily (Matt 16:24). But He took a greater step. He didn't ask everyone to do something He was not willing to do Himself. He literally took up His cross and died on our behalf. He lived the Message. So must we. We must turn to the Lord to receive His lavish grace, that turns our lives and actions into His living Word. Our messages about the love of God are wonderful and true, but those outside of the Kingdom of God say 'don't tell me, show me.' The life of Jesus is captivating and irresistible. Thats why you received Him as your Savior and Lord. A sermon isn't! A sermon can be inspiring and uplifting, but it will not effect people in the streets. But when they see the lifestyle and nature of Jesus operating in their community wherever there are Christians, then it does effect them. They cannot ignore it!

The nails in the ancient keys were placed in a predetermined alignment. Each had to be in the correct place, not just a few of them. All had to be in correct alignment for the key to open the door. Every aspect of Jesus' life had to be in perfect alignment with the Father's. The Messenger, His Message, Motives, Methods, Model and Mission had to be in perfect alignment for the Fathers desire, for the Mess in the Multitudes to be fixed. He is Heaven's blueprint, cornerstone and capstone. The Holy Spirit's work is to bring us all into complete alignment with Him, not just in theory or theology, but in reality.

Realignment To Achieve His Assignment

Every Christian who has been born again, has received the miracle of a transformed life. A divine exchange took place. He who knew no sin, took on sin, so that they who had known sin all their life, could be free of it to live in His perfect righteousness. Christ's blood obliterates sin from all who receive Him as their passover Lamb (Heb Ch 9 &10). This is not a theory, or a theological standpoint that we preach. It is actually what happens the moment someone truly turns from living a life without Jesus Christ, to living for Him, totally by faith in the Son of God.
The Father, Son and Holy Spirit dwell in the spirit of every believer. Your old sinful nature has been replaced with God's righteous nature. Receiving Jesus as your Lord and Savior, was receiving the Master's Key that opened the door deep within you and you were reconciled to God. You and the Father were back dwelling together, in the

garden once again. He has taken up residence and made your heart His home.

When Adam walked with God in the Garden of Eden, we see that a river flowed out of the garden and watered the whole earth, for it to be fruitful (Gen 2:10). What was within the garden was to influence what was outside the garden. It was not God's intension to keep everything within the place of intimacy with Adam and Eve. It was to flow from that place outwards. He wanted the whole earth to be filled with the beauty that was within the garden. God may have taken up residence in your spirit, but He has not done so in order for you to just have a spiritual experience called 'salvation' or have a daily devotional time. He has come to take up residence in your heart to be the eternal wellspring that flows from that place within you, out into your soul, mind, body, your character, your family, finances and the world you live in. This wellspring is described, by Jesus, as "rivers of living water" that will flow out from within you (Jn 7:38).

His presence within you is so powerful, that He will cause everything around Him to come into alignment with His nature and will. The throne of the King of Kings is in the heart of every believer and from this throne of His authority, He will re-order creation. He is not dwelling within the heart of every believer as a holding place until He can get you safely to Heaven. He has turned your heart into His eternal throne and war room! From within you will come His Word of truth, for He is the Truth. His truth will bring revelation to you that will literally transform the way you think, perceive, speak and act. Your life will take on His likeness in order for your life to be His living testimony, a message written not on paper, but etched upon the heart of every believer and out of your heart flow the streams of life (Prov 4:23). He will not stop until you believe and perceive everything as He does. He will not stop until your soul is filled completely with the fruits of the Spirit and your character is transformed to match His. His life within you will begin to invade your body, because He desires it to know complete wholeness, for sickness cannot dwell near Him. It's as if He cannot stop Himself until every person, and all of creation, is saved, healed, made whole, restored into perfect alignment with who He is. He will not stop until all the effects of sin have been eradicated from creation. Of course, the final and complete fulfillment of this will only happen when we eventually all abide in Heaven together. But non-the-less, know this. His persistence and nature will do as much as it can daily, for the rest of your days on earth, for your life to come into complete alignment with Him - the Truth.

This is not the work of man. It is literally the work of God flowing from within you. It has been completely paid for by Jesus, on your behalf. You cannot change yourself. If you could, then you could have saved yourself from being a sinner to being a saint. It is the anointing of God's Spirit that reveals the truth from within you and that revelation will lead you into the manifestation of it.

> *"But the anointing which you have received from Him abides in you, and you do not need that anyone teach you; but as the same anointing teaches you concerning all things, and is true, and is not a lie, and just as it has taught you, you will abide in Him."* (1 John 2:27)

> *"However, when He, the Spirit of truth, has come, He will guide you into all truth;"* (Jn 16:13)

> *"the Spirit of truth, whom the world cannot receive, because it neither sees Him nor knows Him; but you know Him, for He dwells with you and will be in you."* (Jn 14:17)

> *"And you shall know the truth, and the truth shall make you free."* (Jn 8:32)

The Miracle Within You

So many believers are waiting for the anointing to come upon them from Heaven to do a miracle. But He did! Jesus sent Him at Pentecost (Acts 2:1-4). He filled everyone in the upper room. He rests upon every believer because He dwells within every believer. We do not need Him to come down, but come up from within us and flow out of our lives into the world we live in. Your miracle is within your spirit.

God dwells in you and He is the Treasury of Heaven. Jesus, the Key, unlocked the door in order for the treasury of Heaven to fill your life. His Word is Truth and His Truth will set you free from the stinking thinking that has kept you bound, living a life that is less than God provided for and intended you to live. He desires the very best of the very best of the very best for everyone that believes.

You cannot earn it because it was purchased for you already. All He is doing now is getting you to believe the Truth, receive the Truth and the Truth will automatically set you free. Miracles are the by-product of the Truth. But truth challenges everything you have ever known and lived by. So the question is, do you want to keep your stinking thinking, believing the way you always have, or ask God for grace to help you receive and believe His Word is Truth in every situation?

"God dwells in you and He is the Treasury of Heaven."

The Master's Key to your life is to believe that the complete and entire work and cost necessary for you to receive all God's provision for you, was paid for and accomplished by Jesus Christ, the Son of God. It is done. It is finished! He did it for you. When you received Him as your Savior, you received the Master's Key to the entire treasury of God's nature, power and resources, because they reside in Him. He doesn't have them - He is them. When you receive Him, you receive them all. Your very nature changed the moment you received Him into your life. You have been given a new nature;

"Therefore, if anyone is in Christ, he is a new creation; old things have passed away; behold, all things have become new." (2 Cor 5:17)

"that you put off, concerning your former conduct, the old man which grows corrupt according to the deceitful lusts, and be renewed in the spirit of your mind, and that you put on the new man which was created according to God, in true righteousness and holiness." (Eph 4:22-24)

The work of transforming your life into the likeness of Jesus was done the day you accepted Him as your savior and Lord. The work of the Holy Spirit is to renew the spirit of your mind(set) until you see the truth, from the Word of God, which sets you free. The moment you see new truth, the spirit of truth literally invades the whole of your belief system and changes the way you think, perceive and speak. Sometimes the transformation is instantly seen in miraculous ways. Other times it seems to take time to bring the necessary changes. But change you will. This new nature of Christ within you, is called 'The Tree of Life' (Rev 22:1-2). Jesus is called the 'Root and offspring of David' (Rev 22:16). The root produces the fruit. If the root is the nature of God, then the fruits will be the fruits of God. Fruit is the external evidence of the internal life. Don't try to grow the fruit. That's silly. You've never seen a tree 'trying' to grow it's fruit. The fruit is the result of the roots abiding. His presence in you will reproduce itself through you.

So, dear friend, as you read this book, notice I begin every chapter with the same statement. I do so, because my desire is for every believer to grasp that He abides within us all, to bring us into complete alignment with everything it states. Then I believe the life of every believer will become an open portal for Heaven to fill the earth with His likeness.

"But we have this treasure in earthen vessels, that the excellence of the power may be of God and not of us." (2 Cor 4:7)

CHAPTER 2

The Mess

Time For An Apostolic Reformation

When the **MESSENGER** and **MESSAGE** match the **MISSION**, to restore the **MESS** in the chosen **MULTITUDE**, using God's eternal **METHOD**, **MODEL** and **MOTIVATION**, delivered at the **MOMENT** of His prompting, it brings supernatural **MULTIPLICATION** and the realignment of all things, into His likeness.

"In the beginning God created the heavens and the earth. The earth was without form, and void, and darkness was on the face of the deep. And the Spirit of God was hovering over the face of the waters." (Gen 1:1)

Devastated, grief-stricken, because her only son was void of life, a mother walked amongst the procession of family and friends, who carried the coffin of her dead son. The emotional pain a person feels when the light of life has gone out of their loved one, is beyond describable words. The emptiness they feel at that moment is a reflection of the body inside the coffin. The life that was meant to be filled with light, has now been reduced to darkness. The dreams of a mother are now it seems not to be. Her plans and thoughts of a wonderful future are in a mess! (Luke 7:11-17).

Jesus, sees the procession, is moved with compassion and intervenes. He looks into the coffin, touches it and speaks to the young man to live. Instantly, this body, just a few minutes earlier, void of life, suddenly sits up and speaks. I would love to have known the subject of this boy's first words!
This miracle reflects the very first verses of the Bible. God's creation had become a Mess. The light had been replaced with darkness. What had been filled with life, was void of it. But the Spirit of God hovered over the scene. The compassion of God for His creation brought Him right into the situation. He was moved to respond. He hovered and spoke;

"Let there be light." (Gen 1:3)

Thick darkness may have filled the situation and everything may have looked impossible to be any different. But the moment God came and spoke with compassion, there would only be one outcome. Light began to shatter the grip of this darkness, rolling it back so that what had been covered over, was now exposed. Creation experienced a resurrection, because our God is the God of Life, and death cannot contain Him. The widow of Nain, Mary, the apostles, and Lazarus all encountered Him. He is alive and is moved by so much compassion, that He will intervene, even at the point when hope is all but gone.

God's Answer To The Dilemma - A New Man

Once He refashioned the earth and life was flourishing, God then created a man to tend it and keep it the way it was meant to be. His answer to protecting and keeping the earth in His intended condition, was a man. He created an environment called the Garden of Eden and then fashioned the man perfectly suited to keep the environment God's intended way. Adam was created with a purpose and had a function. His purpose was to be a worshipper. His function, to fulfill God's will and rule on His behalf.

God created a garden in which He and Adam walked together in intimate relationship. Out of this garden flowed the rivers of water that would constantly replenish the whole earth. Everything created derived it's life and fruitfulness from God, and it flowed because of Adam's relationship with Him in this garden.

Adams role was to be more than a mere gardener or farmer. His role was much more pivotal than that. God fashioned him, placing within him every gift and ability he would need to fulfill the task given him. It is vital today, that we understand this truth from the outset of this apostolic message of reformation. To keep everything the way God intended, God fashioned a man and gave him the relationship and abilities he needed to achieve God's required commission. Everything flowed out of that garden of intimacy. Everything in creation found it's correct place and alignment as long as Adam stayed in correct alignment to that place of intimacy with God. God was, and still is, the very source of life for all creation. He is the Key to everything working correctly.

The relationship man has with Him is described by Jesus as the vine and it's branches (John 15). As long as the branch is connected to the vine, the root source of it's life, then the life in the root flows through the branch and becomes fruitful. Disconnection from the root terminates it's life-source and brings eventual decay and death to the the branch. Man, the vehicle created of God to release the potential of His life into this creation, would be unable to fulfill his function.

When Adam and Eve (together called 'man' - Gen 2:26) allowed themselves to yield to Lucifer's temptation, they stepped away from their Heaven given assignment and a Mess flooded into the earth once again. Therefore, the way to bring everything back into alignment with God's intension is to fashion a new 'Adam' who would not succumb to sin, but remain in His assigned place and faithfully fulfill the command of God. We know of course, this new Adam is Jesus Christ. But Jesus was also known as the 'Seed' of God and a seed reproduces it's likeness.

Jesus was both wholly God and wholly man, come into the earth as the Redeeming One, who fully paid the ransom to end the curse of sin and death for all mankind and fix the Mess. Jesus was faithful even unto death. But in His loins He carried the seed of a new breed of 'man' made in His likeness. Neither male nor female, Jew or Gentile, but one 'new man.' A new creation (2Cor 5:17/Gal 6:15).

"A tree is known by it's fruit, not it's height, width or depth."

This 'New Man' is the 'corporate man,' the many membered Body of Christ (1 Cor 12:12-14). At Pentecost (Acts 2), the Spirit of God was poured out and given to men. The Spirit of God is now within every member of this 'new man,' thus revealing this many membered body is the body of Jesus, the 2nd Adam (Col 1:18).

There may be darkness across the globe, but God has His 'man' in the earth. This 'man' of God is the Church, made up of male, female, black, white, young, old, all who are born again and called by His Name. This Body of Jesus is connected to both Heaven and earth at the same time (Eph 1:10). He only has one body, one Church and one Kingdom. The work of the Spirit of God is to connect it all and keep it connected, in order for God's life to flow into this earth in it's fullest measure.

Lucifer's strategy in the Garden of Eden was to simply disconnect Adam and Eve from their relationship and fellowship with God. He succeeded. Adam and Eve were removed from the garden of intimacy, a gate was closed and two Cherub angels with flaming swords, placed at the gate to stop man re-entering in their sinful state (Gen 3:24). But the moment you accept Jesus as your personal Savior, the gate swings wide open again and you are restored to intimacy with the Father.

Now the strategy of the kingdom of darkness changes. It does not have the power to disconnect this new 'Adam' because the work of Jesus was eternal, total, complete. Nothing can now separate you from the love of Christ (Rom 8:35). But it will try to disrupt the fellowship you have with God, keep you disconnected from the rest of the Body of Christ, in order to limit the measure of God's ability being released into the earth. He has done such a good job at deceiving the Church, that we have churches and denominations preaching against unity with other parts of the Church, due to theological differences. My response to this is simple. Your own theology cannot be perfect theology if it opposes the command or character of God. Look at these Bible verses;

"This is My commandment, that you love one another as I have loved you." (John 15:12).

Did He require us to have perfect theology before He saved us and came to dwell within us? No! He knew you could not have perfect understanding. Why then demand of others what God does not demand of you?

"Owe no one anything except to love one another, for he who loves another has fulfilled the law." (Rom 8:13)

The basis of the law is love, not perfection. No-one has fellowship with God based upon perfection, but upon His love and acceptance. He has made you perfect through His own sacrifice. How can a Christian, saved and in relationship with God by His grace, not offer fellowship with other believers on this same basis?

> *"But concerning brotherly love you have no need that I should write to you, for you yourselves are taught by God to love one another;" (1 Thess 4:9)*

It seems more important to God to teach love, than a lot of other theologies. Maybe it should be for us also.

> *"For this is the message that you heard from the beginning, that we should love one another," (1 John 3:11)*

John, the apostle, mentions that they received this teaching about love 'from the beginning.' Not half-way through their time with Jesus, but from the outset. In other words the apostles believed this whole message of loving one another the way God loved them, was paramount and foundational, that every other thing be built on top of this understanding.

> *"By this all will know that you are My disciples, if you have love for one another." (John 13:35)*

A tree is known by it's fruit, not it's height, width or depth. Fruit is the external evidence of an internal life. If you don't love and like people, then how can you say you love God, because He loves them as much as He loves you. How can you say the love of God is in you, if you don't love others as He loves you? The amount of people in meetings, the size of a building, the popularity of a preacher, the style of a worship service, are not the 'fruit' the Spirit is trying to bear in and through His Church. You can have all the above and yet never evidence the fruit and gifts of the Spirit, which are the evidence and testimony of the God who dwells within. I am concerned how few congregations are being taught what the gifts of the Spirit are and how to let them flow through their lives. Teaching the Church to bear the fruit of the Spirit, but not the gifts of the Spirit is like a tree having foliage but no fruit, or giving a person a building trade but no power tools to work with.

"Finally, all of you be of one mind, having compassion for one another; love as brothers, be tenderhearted, be courteous;" (1Pet 3:8)

Peter, through this one statement, calls the whole Church to have the same mind and spirit. He asks all of us to have compassion for one another and love as brothers.

I have siblings. I love them dearly, but I don't always agree with them, nor they with me. My love for them is not dependent upon whether they say what I say and do what I do. My love for them is because we have the same father. It is unconditional. It makes no demand upon the other person to be in agreement with me for me to love them. I love my brothers and sister because God taught it to me and because they are my family, meaning we have the same father. The Body of Christ has but one Father of all (Eph 4:4-6). It is His desire, and instruction, that there be an atmosphere in His house, that matches His character, which is unconditional love.

You Are Here On Purpose, With a Purpose

God knew you from before the foundations of the world and formed you in your mothers womb when it was time for you to be born. You arrived on purpose, with a purpose! No matter if anyone said you were a mistake, or not expected, you are Heavens **Messenger**, with a **Message**, which is the solution to earth's **Mess**.

When Adam stepped away from his God given assignment, he did more than just disobey God. He shredded the blueprint of God, believing his plan was better than the Father's. This blind and prideful attitude opened a spiritual door into his life, that he had no idea existed. Darkness, death, unbelief and guilt flooded into His life, effecting all mankind. From that moment onwards mankind was flooded with a darkness God never desired man to ever know. Adam and Eve's error would now release death and devastation upon all who followed after them. Our disregard and disobedience effects not just ourselves, but our children and children's children, because our lives act like a door in the spirit realm.

Church history is littered with this same sad storyline. When the Church comes into alignment with their heavenly assignment, then the light of the gospel begins to fill the earth. Whenever the Church rejects God's blueprint, instead desiring to operate a clever man made, man centered, man controlled system, then history records that she becomes visionless, passionless and powerless to reach the world with the love of Christ. Instead she becomes insular, isolated, institutionalized and irrelevant to the society she is meant to reach. Eventually, the Church, the people God intended to use to bring His solution to the Mess, evolve instead into nothing more than a teaching center, educating millions of people with knowledge about a God that they really don't know. If they knew Him, then they would be unable to stay inside cleverly designed buildings, carefully following the rules of Church life. If they really knew Him, then they would be about their Father's business, which is not theological education, but the restoration of all things (Acts 3:21) through the impartation of His love, life and forgiveness.

Jesus, the God we say we so passionately serve, built no earthly building or institution, no Bible School and wrote no books. He carried no dvd's of His messages, needed no worship team, or platform with smoke and special lighting effects. He wore no special garments, or crosses around His neck. He had no earthly degree, ordination papers, which confirmed He was authenticated by a theological denomination. He did not have His own TV, radio program or website with weekly podcasts. Yet, He touched the hearts of His generation within 3 years and has done so to every generation since.

The only building He concerned Himself with was the eternal Temple of God made out of living stones. He wrote no book, yet the Book of God, the Bible, written by 66 individuals, each inspired by the Holy Spirit, is Him entirely. He needed no dvd or film crews, His action at Calvary is impregnated into history and forever in the hearts of those who have met Him and received Him into their lives as Savior and Lord. The angelic hosts were His worship team, who gathered in their thousands in the unseen realms around Him at all times. He could see and hear their voices filling Heaven and creation with His praises. The only platform He has ever needed is the one provided by those who responded to the sound of His voice calling their name. He comes, and sits and dines with them personally, every day they desire. So close, He need not shout from a mountain top, He can simply whisper within them and they hear His intimate voice quietly reassuring, leading and illuminating them.

An Invitation To Know Jesus

Dear reader, I need to ask you a question before we close this chapter. Do you know this Jesus I am talking about? Not do you know about Him because you have attended a Church. Do you have a personal intimate relationship with Him right now? Have you invited Him to be your Savior and Lord? If you say 'Wynne, I am not sure.' then it is safe for me to say you haven't. Anyone born again knows without a shadow of a doubt, that He is in their life.

If you are unsure, or have never received Jesus into your life, then do so now before we go any further. Simply talk to Him right now. Say this prayer out load;

Father, I come to you today in the Name of Jesus Christ Your Son. I want to confess that I have lived without knowing you personally in my life. I have never made you my Savior and Lord, but I wish to do so right now. I ask you to forgive me of all my sin, known or unknown. I ask that the blood of Jesus cleanse my conscience of all sin and ask that you give me His righteousness.

I thank you that today you hear my prayer and I will, from this day on, believe you love me completely, have forgiven me and made your home in me. I will, for the rest of my life, believe that the perfect work of Jesus has made me acceptable to you, my Heavenly Father.

I ask for your Holy Spirit to fill me with your eternal life and grant me, by grace, the ability to live in the fullness of all you have provided for me to walk in, through the death and resurrection of Jesus. I ask by your grace, that you will help me know you more, love and honor you, and serve your purposes for the rest my life.

CHAPTER 3

The Metamorphasis!

New Wine, New Wineskin

When the **MESSENGER** and **MESSAGE** match the **MISSION**, to restore the **MESS** in the chosen **MULTITUDE**, using God's eternal **METHOD**, **MODEL** and **MOTIVATION**, delivered at the **MOMENT** of His prompting, it brings supernatural **MULTIPLICATION** and the realignment of all things, into His likeness.

At a point in it's life, a caterpillar crawls along a branch and begins to fashion around itself a chrysalis, in order to metamorphosis into a butterfly. It is hard to imagine the beautiful butterfly began as a caterpillar, because it has changed so much through the process. The transformation releases the butterfly to use ability it never expressed as a caterpillar. No longer clinging to branches, moving slowly, it now uses wings to fly from plant to plant with a new expression and array of color. The metamorphosis is a wonderful illustration of the Christians life and the life of the Church. The caterpillar died and was transformed into something completely different - a butterfly, a completely different life-form. It can no longer be what it once was. It cannot go back to being the caterpillar.

It must go through transformation and metamorphosis to accomplish it's purpose and destiny. The transformation challenges us to learn to use new ways to do the work of God. We cannot remain the way we are. Everything is changing. If you do not change, then you will become a spiritual 'fossil,' a picture of something that once had a powerful life it no longer has. Dear friend, don't be afraid to change.

"If you do not change, then you will become a spiritual 'fossil.'"

The present model of Church so often experienced today, is not accomplishing the task of reaching the 7.3 billion people presently alive in the earth. It never can do. We need a real transformation, reformation and metamorphosis in understanding who we are, what we are here to do and how to do it. Our present world is rapidly changing, faster than we can comprehend. Whilst much of the global Church either doesn't see the necessity of changing, or is afraid to make the changes. Many make what I call superficial and cosmetic changes, but the actual underlying foundational principles and spirit of the Church doesn't change at all. So we end up just getting a church that looks younger and radical, which still doesn't achieve the real purpose of it's existence.

Changing the look of a platform, casting aside the suits and ties, exchanging the organ and choir with a rock band, does not mean the Church has truly changed at all. It may be more relevant to reach a younger generation, which is great, but if the core concept of the Church does not go through metamorphosis, then the new Church will look old in twenty years time and will still have not accomplished the goal it exists for, in the mind of God.

What For? What Then?

When a young couple come to me to say they are getting married, I always ask them 'what for?' Of course their answer is that they love each other. I continue to ask them, 'what happens when you don't feel that way? What then?' There's more to a marriage than getting married. Most of these young couples have never thought any further than the wedding ceremony. Their focus was upon an event called a marriage service, thinking the service and actual marriage where somehow the same thing. But there is a reason to get married and it is so much deeper and meaningful than to just be together in the same house. The marriage ceremony is but the first step of a long journey with a destiny in mind. The destiny is not the length of years they dwell together, but the manifestation of what true love looks like within their relationship.

Young ministers tell me they are going to plant a church, or start a ministry. I ask them the same two questions - 'What for?' and 'What then?' Starting a Church or ministry is exactly that - a starting point. But if we do not know the purpose of God for doing it, then we will probably simply reproduce what everyone else is reproducing around us.

I wish to ask you some questions. Why did Jesus save you? Why did He fill you with Himself? Why are you alive right now in this generation? You gave your heart to Jesus - what for? You read your

Bible, pray, attend a church group - what for?

We are not meant to do any of these things because they are 'the right thing to do!' We must grasp the purpose of His life being in us and therefore the purpose of our life. We need to ask ourselves questions like, What is the Church? Where should it be? What should it be doing? What time should it meet? What should it look or sound like? What am I meant to be in it?

The Church was birthed with explosive life in an upper room 2000 years ago. The Book of Acts records the powerful way the Holy Spirit led Church swept through nations impacting lives, cities, cultures everywhere they went. Signs and wonders were normal. Historians tells us that over 100 million people came into the Kingdom of God in the first 100 years. Their presence challenged governments, dictators, the religious, business and social world. Society was transformed with the love of Jesus because they lived out the culture of the Kingdom of God everywhere they went. They lived, not to please themselves, believing the world owed them something. They lived to please God knowing the world offered them nothing, because what they had was much greater than what the world could give them.
They lived with the attitude to do whatever it took to spread the message of God's redeeming love and forgiveness. They readily gave up homes and dreams in order to take His love to another city, region or country. The whole Church lived for this purpose. All their talents, gifts, abilities and possessions were utilized for this end. They did not waste one ounce of energy, or waste finances on anything that did not have this ultimate goal at it's core. They reached people, converted them to Christ. They discipled them and then sent them out to do likewise. They didn't need the biggest Church building in town to do it! They had no Church programs to commit too. They were committed not to building Church, but seeking first the Kingdom of God and His righteousness, in the hearts of all people. They knew the reason Jesus gave them a spiritual metamorphosis. It was to know Christ intimately and make Him known to everyone, not just through words, but by living and revealing the culture of His

Kingdom in the earth, wherever they were.

If this is the New Testament mandate laid down by Jesus and the apostles, then it is to be ours also. If our life, ministry or Church is not in alignment with this mandate and is simply just 'doing church,' then we need to ask some more questions. "What do we need to do?" "What do we need to change, to do so?" Then make the changes.

The Enemy Within

Everything God creates reproduces itself organically (in the natural way). It does not need an organization to help it! The Church is birthed of God, therefore, it has an inherent ability to automatically reproduce His kind of life. Yet, so often Churches are stifled, stunted and stagnant, decreasing in size and effectiveness. Something is wrong and it is not because we are under the attack of the devil! Nor is it because the spirit of secularism is at work in society turning hearts against the gospel. NOTHING can prevent, or overcome the power of His resurrection life filling this earth with His glory, except the unbelief and traditions of men (Matt 15:6). The problem is not outside the Church, it is within her.

"The problem is not outside the Church, it is within her. "

Gwenda and I travel all over the world speaking in thousands of Church meetings and leaders gatherings. We find ourselves in the privileged position of being people trusted by many who desire to share their deepest concerns about Church life as they experience it. The message is loud and clear from leaders to congregations, from pastors to traveling ministries. Everyone says the same. They 'joined up' to the Kingdom of God with great joy and expectancy, to do something that would change their world with the love and grace of

God. They were excited to think that God would use them in some similar way that he used the disciples in the New Testament. But, their dreams and hopes of those early days differ drastically from their present reality. They honestly, almost apologetically, say to us that now after many years of serving God and the Church faithfully, they are bored with Church and just wish they could go and do ....
and right there in front of us, out spills their long held dream and desires which they have never been released or enabled to do, because of the religious 'system' they find themselves held captive by.

Make sure you don't misunderstand what was just said. They are not bored with Jesus or His Kingdom purposes. They still love His people. They are just bored with the endless pressure to attend more and more meetings and are looked upon as being 'uncommitted' if they do not come to everything the Church does, preferring instead to put their families needs first, or just have some down time to fulfill a hobby or a personal dream. They are tired of Church politics, control mechanisms, broken promises and the pain involved in being part of Church life. I am serious, these are the words of leaders and congregations spoken to us endlessly wherever we go.

When so many of the 'family' we are meant to have an incredible loving relationship with, just desire to give up because of all the 'stuff' of Church life, and no longer want involvement in what we are doing, then we must ask ourselves a question. What have we done with what He gave us? He gave us a life, not an organization. He gave us His life, but we have turned it into an institution.

Obsolete & Fading Away

"In that He says "a new covenant," He has made the old obsolete. Now what is becoming obsolete and growing old is ready to vanish away." (Heb 8:13)

"He takes away the first that He may establish the second." (Heb 10:9)

I sincerely believe the model of Church life as we have known it, is being changed from all we have ever known to something we have never experienced before. There is a new wineskin for a new wine being poured out and the Church fights over an old piece of cloth that once served it's purpose.

Everything God created in our world has a beginning and an end. It is life's cycle. As something dies, something new is birthed. I urge you to not fight over what is fading away, even though once upon a time it was glorious. Instead, let us trust God to clothe us with something new and reveal an even greater expression of His glory, which will in turn glorify Him even more and give millions of new believers experiences that create a new wave of memories that tell of the goodness of God in the land of the living.

"How Do You Make The Church Grow?" ### Is The Wrong Question!

When a baby is born you never see the midwife grab its head, the nurse grab its legs and both pull the baby in opposite directions to make it grow. In fact you would scream for them to stop, wondering what kind of health institution would have this practice. A baby doesn't grow by such a method. It grows because growth is built into every cell of it's being. It is a natural process coming from within, not from outside. You may have a "vision" or a "goal" for your child to be six feet tall, 250lbs in weight and be a top professional basketball player. But visions and goals do not make a baby grow. Nor do they make the Church or a ministry grow!

You cannot 'make' a baby grow. You don't need too. A new born baby has all it needs within itself to grow. It doesn't grow just because you feed it. Within the child lies a multitude of cells, organs, nerve endings, blood, a digestive system and millions of other parts all miraculously working together. You cannot see them or their workings, but you can see their effects. All these parts working together in an optimum way, allow the child to grow, develop and function in life to the maximum. All of these things work because of one thing. A baby grows because of the life that resides within them. The cell-life within them reproduces. It is this rapid reproduction and multiplication of cells that makes a child grow. Goals just help us raise up a child and give direction to what to do with their life. They do not make a child grow.

If there is no life in the very first cell, then it cannot reproduce. It is only capable of multiplying and growing because of the life that dwells within it.

Jesus is 'abundant' Life (John 10:10). And we must grasp this truth. Life produces growth not vice versa. It is the very life of God that makes the Church grow, not it's programs. Whatever life is in the original cell is what gets multiplied. God's life is eternal and heavenly. Man's is not. You may have a Church full of activity and programs, but is Heaven's life being reproduced or the life of an earthly institution and organization?

Church Growth Is Not Numerical Growth.

If you remove the very essence of the life of God from the Church, the Church will die. It cannot live. It cannot reproduce and will not grow. Asking a Church to grow and be fruitful without recognizing it is the life of the Spirit that makes it grow, is like asking the body of a man without life in it, to live. It is simply impossible. Anytime man throws out the working of the Spirit, the work once named 'a movement' becomes a monument. Just like a fossil is evidence of something that once lived and roamed, but has no life or ability to do so now.

Church growth in the eyes of God is not evidenced by numerical people on seats. Church growth is quantified by the personal growth and fruitfulness, of every individual believer. When one believer grows up in God and reproduces that life, then and only then can we declare the Church grew. It is time we stopped living in the foolishness of focusing on numbers in meetings and attended to individual growth, which is exactly what Jesus did in the beginning. Don't try to make the Church grow. Instead, realign the Church, which allows for the life of the Spirit to freely flow. Life produces life. Jesus began with twelve individual men called 'disciples. He taught, trained and turned them into apostles, who were enabled to do what He did. He reproduced Himself. To reproduce Him in others today, must be my desire also.

Institutionalized, Internalized and Impotent!

When first saved, I was so full of joy that I told everyone about Jesus and my salvation. I knew almost nothing theologically, yet I led over 200 people to find salvation in Christ in one year. I read that if I laid hands on the sick they would recover. So I did it. Miracles and healing's happened almost every day. The more I shared my testimony, the more God kept using me to reproduce new believers. Wow, it was so simple. Before I knew where I was, I was holding meetings in homes and halls, bringing the presence of Jesus through sharing His Word for all to understand and it all kept growing.
I don't mean this in some egotistical way, just as a question. What would happen if every new believer was encouraged to operate like this? It would be just like it was in the early years of the birth of the Church. It would be exploding everywhere, like wild-fires, uncontrollable, self igniting and propelling.

The Church so often stunts it's potential to grow because it intervenes in the natural process God uses. Therefore we get more and more institutionalized, internalized and impotent. Man reproduces man. Flesh produces more flesh. Earthly creates earthly kind of life, whilst heavenly life produces heavenly life.
Being 'born again' means 'born from above,' referring from Heaven. The 'heavenly' is birthed within you for the purpose of reproduction. Heaven desires to fill the earth with the same life Heaven enjoys. When the Church operates using the same practices, philosophies and principles of earthly institutions and businesses, then the only outcome will be more of the same. It is time to break the mould. It is time to get off this treadmill of going in circles (the sign of Israel's

disobedience) using lots of energy and effort that bear so little fruit and return to the place where Heaven is freely being revealed in earth.

'Alignment For Assignment' is a call to battle. It contains an eternal battle plan that can change every person and nation. It reveals interconnecting things needing to be discipled into every believer, in order for their understanding of Kingdom life to be lived and to keep us in alignment with God's heavenly blueprint, which of course is His Son Jesus. Each chapter is a piece of the picture that must be connected and kept in balance by the others, just like the wheels in a watch and the hundreds of parts within an engine.

I believe God is waiting to pour out His power like we have never seen before and it will only truly be released when the Church is perfectly aligned with the Head of the Church. It is imperative we understand this message for we are the doorkeepers of God's treasury in the earth.

CHAPTER 4

The Mission

Alignment For Assignment

When the **MESSENGER** and **MESSAGE** match the **MISSION**, to restore the **MESS** in the chosen **MULTITUDE**, using God's eternal **METHOD, MODEL** and **MOTIVATION**, delivered at the **MOMENT** of His prompting, it brings supernatural **MULTIPLICATION** and the realignment of all things, into His likeness.

His Vision Is My Mission

When the sight of a gun is out of alignment, then it wouldn't matter how great the manufacturing and design of the gun is, how precise the bullet has been fashioned, or how talented the rifleman is - the bullet will not hit the target! The sight of a gun is the equivalent to the vision and mission of a Christian. The way I view the difference between vision and mission is simple. His vision is my mission. This makes the vision eternal and spiritual and our mission earthly and temporal. God's vision has never changed. It is built upon eternal principles and values. The mission is how we achieve the establishing of His vision, in our generation and culture. This means it must be adapted in order to achieve it's end in differing cultures, nations, generations and situations.

The Kingdom of God is eternal, heavenly and spiritual. The work of the Church is earthly and temporal. The work the Church is called to do on earth will one day end. But the Kingdom of God will never end. The way we present or communicate the gospel can change from generation to generation, nation to nation, culture to culture. But the actual message, power, values, culture and purpose of the gospel never change. They are the same yesterday, today and forever.

If our vision is not in alignment with the Savior's, then we will not hit the target and achieve His destiny. We may see wonderful meetings and events, but we will not see His glory fully manifest in our generation, the way He desires. Our mission in life must align itself with His eternal vision. Jesus said;

"Seek first the Kingdom of God and His righteousness and all these things shall be added to you." (Matt 6:33)

If you seek the Kingdom of God you will obtain the Church. If you seek the Church, it does not necessarily mean you achieve the result of gaining His Kingdom. Our emphasis must be to 'root' the understanding and establishment of God's Kingdom in the heart of every believer from the moment of their commitment to Christ. Only then will we reap the fruit of the Kingdom. If you root a plant in good soil, then you will automatically gain the fruit because the fruit is the byproduct. The Church is not the root, the Kingdom is, because He is the King and His Kingdom is the manifestation of His character and attributes. The Kingdom is just like the King. We, the Church, must create the culture of God's Kingdom principles in the hearts of people everywhere.

Our world today is filled with a myriad of denominations, streams, networks, independent Churches, Church splits and ministries, each believing they have the fuller understanding of what God is saying and doing today. The evidence of so much dis-unity is sadly the result of simply rooting 'Church' instead of 'Kingdom' into the hearts of new believers. When you are 'Church' rooted, then everything revolves around the theology, policies and the vision of the Church or denomination you are rooted in. When the Kingdom is rooted in you, then you have a desire to build the culture of the Kingdom of God everywhere, not just within your 'stream' or individual Church group, because it is based upon the revelation of His heart, not our interpretation of the Bible, or our 'style' of Church.

The culture of God's Kingdom on earth, is no different than it is in Heaven. Heaven's culture is relational based, not theological. It is Father centered, not man centered. It does not have walls that keep the family divided, it is all inclusive. A ministry or Church stream may have a 'candle' of revelation to burn, but in the Kingdom Jesus is the complete Light. Isolated and alone, churches and ministries have just a tiny glimmer of revelation of Him and operate in a lack of light and revelation. But when side by side, adding each revelation to each others, we become a candelabra instead of a single candle. We cannot afford to be divided when so much is dependent upon this world seeing His Kingdom come.

When our emphasis is not upon the eternal principles and purposes of God's Kingdom, then we will always descend to operating and focussing upon the temporal issues of Church life and preference, which, in the fulness of time, will fade away. The word 'kingdom' is made from the two words, 'king' and 'domain.' If Jesus is truly our King and His will has dominion in our lives, then His will has become our will and His purposes and culture will be seen reflected in our purposes and culture. You cannot have His Kingdom without the acceptance of His will. They come together. So it is simple. Look at the global Church and it's history and see whose kingdom is operating, by the very fruit we produce. Wherever the Kingdom is operating, we will find the fruit and gifts of the Spirit flowing freely. In my humble opinion, the Church 'tree' is laden with the fruit of the Church 'system,' not the fruit of the Spirit or Kingdom of God. If what I say is correct, then we need a global shift in emphasis away from Church goals, to Kingdom vision and mission.

"Jesus is not going to return for a religious institution or system."

Let me ask one more question. How much of our Church income is directed to ministry and mission work outside of our four walls? How much of it is allocated to Church expenses, buildings or meetings?

When I was the chief leader in the Church, we gave 10% of all our income to mission and ministry work outside of our Church. I thought I was operating a good thing until in the final years of pastoring in Wales, I sensed the Lord show me it would be better the other way around. Could I believe and restructure so that we could operated on the 10% and give the 90% to fulfilling His vision outside of our building? It will take a major shift in Church thinking to see this happen in our lifetime. But the world is never reached or changed by doing 'the same ol same ol,' or by mediocre people. It is influenced by radical and passionate people. We need radical passionate Kingdom minded believers who are focused and driven to fulfill Heaven's purpose of seeing His Kingdom come in earth, more than obtaining obedience to imperfect theology or the size of a congregation. Striving for excellent theology is necessary and a good thing, but it is not a condition for God to use you. A willing heart to serve His purposes is sufficient.

This Same Jesus

"Men of Galilee, why do you stand gazing up into Heaven? This same Jesus, who was taken up from you into Heaven, will so come in like manner as you saw Him go into Heaven." (Acts 1:11)

It seems to me that God is a very precise person. He knows exactly what He wants to achieve and exactly how He desires to achieve it. In communicating with His people, He seems to always give them detailed patterns or blueprints to accomplish His plan.

He gave clear and precise instructions to Adam in Eden. He gave Noah detailed plans for the Ark, to Moses for the Tabernacle, to David for his Tabernacle and for Solomon's Temple. To Nehemiah, He gave the vision of how to rebuild the city of Jerusalem and to John, the apostle, He gave a clear vision, with dimensions, about the New Jerusalem (Rev 22). If this is His pattern of operating, then it must be the way He would do it today, for the Church to be realigned to all He is and is doing.

In Acts 1: 11, the disciples were gazing up watching Jesus ascend into the clouds and were distracted by the appearance of two angelic beings. The angels asked the disciples 'why do you stand gazing up into Heaven.' Well, wouldn't you if your friend, pastor, or anyone for that matter, was talking with you, suddenly said a quick farewell and started to ascend into the atmosphere? They were watching Jesus do something absolutely outside of their boxes of 'normality.' Their eyes were probably on stalks and their jaws wide open at the sight and were straining their eyes into the bright sunlit sky, no doubt not wanting to miss that final moment of His disappearing. Suddenly, their focus is disturbed by the words of these angels;

*"This **same** Jesus who was taken up into Heaven, will so come in like manner as you saw Him go into Heaven."*

Whilst reading this passage one morning I suddenly saw something I had never noticed before. The translators of the Bible had inserted the word 'same' in italics, which means the actual word is not in the original Greek writing of the book of Acts, but is a word the translators used to get the meaning of the phrase across to the reader in the best grammatical format.

I was fully aware the Body of Christ primarily, had taken the meaning of this verse to be referring to how Jesus would return in the same 'manner,' meaning the same way He left, in the clouds. I am not wishing to start an argument of whether Jesus will come in the clouds or not, because I actually couldn't care if He came on the clouds, in a chariot, on horseback or in a jet, as long as He returns. But I don't believe Luke wrote these words to emphasize the mode of how Jesus will return. I think the emphasis the angels were making was on the nature of the person of Jesus and His manner of life, not the manner of transport used to ascend and descend.

"This *same* Jesus" is a pretty absurd thing to say to His disciples if the focus of the conversation was all about the manner of transport used for His return. The angels were not confused. They knew exactly what they were sent to do. They were simply reminding the disciples to keep focused on this same resurrected Jesus, because it is this one that is Heaven's blueprint and pattern, not the one who was birthed, lived for thirty-three years, was crucified and died. The one they were to copy was the resurrected one who knew no limitations. The one that death could not contain. The one who walls could not keep Him out or in. The one that appeared and reappeared in different 'forms.' This is the one who will return. And they must make sure to do everything possible to lay down the guidelines and foundations for the Church to be built according to this Heavenly pattern.

Just as with Noah, Moses and all the others, given His plans and blueprints, these apostles were getting clear, precise instructions on what to build and how to build it.

For six weeks, Jesus had spent every moment necessary with them, instructing them. Not once does the narrative refer to Him teaching them how to build buildings, take offerings, lead a prayer meeting or any such thing. Nowhere does it record His telling them the 'where' and 'hows' of what they were going to do. It is clear, to me, the emphasis was on the Kingdom of God (Acts 1:3). Jesus is not going to return for a religious institution or system. He is not coming back for a denomination, a stream, or a group built around a specific set of doctrines (although I fully believe in having good Biblical doctrine). He is coming back for a Bride, His family, a people just like Himself.

When a man and woman get married and set up a home, their major concern when raising children, is the family atmosphere and core values. If you have a son who is arrogant, divisive, unclean and disrespectful to you and your friends, then it matters little to you that he is brilliant academically. What matters most to you is the family atmosphere or lack of it. His academic quality is wonderful. But if through his poor character he destroys the unity of the family, then you instantly begin to bring the changes necessary so that the loving and respectful family atmosphere you desire is produced. It is not his head that you are most concerned with, but his heart. "By this love will all men know you are My disciples" is not a head, but a heart issue. Our relationship with Him and others seems more important to Jesus, than our complete and accurate account of Him. To **know** Him is more essential than to know **about** Him.

Filled With The Glory of God

In the final two chapters of the Bible, John, the apostle, writes of the New Jerusalem coming down out of Heaven. He describes it's beauty. He mentions that there will be no Temple needed, because Lord God and the Lamb will be the Temple. He describes in verses 9 and 10 that the New Jerusalem is the Bride of Christ (the Church). All the way through Chapter 22 he describes the city. In the midst of it all he writes;

> *"The city had no need of the sun or of the moon to shine in it, for **the glory of God** illuminated it." Rev 21:23*

It would be so easy to simply read over this without absorbing the depth of it's meaning. The glory of God is His likeness, or character (read Ex 33:21-22; Ch 34:6-7). The New Jerusalem, the Church, will not need a building to house the glory of God as revealed in the Old Testament, but the glory will fill the streets and homes. He never desired His glory to be kept within a building, He has always desired it to fill the earth. He never desired for His glory just to reside in you, but to be such a natural expression of who He is in you, that it manifest out through you in life, everywhere you are. He wants it revealed out in the streets, the highways of normal life.

Dear friend, let us grasp this is the way God wants it today. We are already living in His eternal life. We don't need to wait until we get to Heaven to live it. The day we were born again we entered into it. We can see it work out in our lives here on earth. He desires to transform each of us to reveal His likeness in us here, not when we get to Heaven;

> *"that you put off, concerning your former conduct, the old man which grows corrupt according to deceitful lusts, and be renewed in the spirit of your mind, and that you put on the new man which was created according to God, in true righteousness and holiness." (Eph 4:23-24)*

Now let us read these verses in a different translation, the New Living Testament, so we can see it's fuller meaning;

> *"throw off your old sinful **nature** and your former way of life, which is corrupted by lust and deception. Instead, let the Spirit renew your thoughts and attitudes. Put on your **new nature, created to be like God**—truly righteous and holy."*

The new nature is the one you received at your conversion to Christ. It is the 'new man,' also referred to as the 'new creation.' (Gal 6:15)

Again, in the Book to the Galatians it states;

> *"But we **all**, with unveiled face, beholding as in a mirror the glory of the Lord, are being **transformed into the same image** from glory to glory, just as by the Spirit of the Lord." (2Cor 3:18)*

The glory kept within the Old Testament Temple, exploded to life outside it's walls and into the streets, through the life and ministry of Jesus, 2000 years ago. Then He gave to the Church His Spirit at Pentecost, to enable and empower us, not just to do the works of the Spirit, but for our lives to also reveal His glory and image. The spiritual transformation done within us on the day we were saved, He desires to be outworked for all to see. His glory is to be revealed in our heart and soul, but also in our body, relationships, marriages and homes. In fact in every area of our lives.

Remember, Jesus is not a dictator. He came into your life because you desired Him too. The supernatural nature and life of God resides within you. But He will not just overtake your life and make His glory manifest through you. You must want it and seek Him for it and it will flow and transform all of your life. You are not now born of earth. You are born from above. You have been given the nature of God, His DNA. It is time for every believer to grasp what He has given them. This new nature is nothing like the old one that was crucified in Christ;

> *"I have been crucified with Christ; it is no longer I who live, but Christ lives in me; and the life which I now live in the flesh I live by faith in the Son of God," (Gal 2:20)*

If crucified with Him, then this old sinful nature of mine is gone. It is dead and buried in Christ and I was raised in His resurrection life. As He ascended, then I ascended with Him and am now seated in Him at the right hand of the Father (Rom 6:4/Eph 2:5-6). I am seated, by faith, in Him upon the throne of God. I am given this place to rule and reign over sin, to walk in the power of His Spirit and to reveal His transforming nature in this world.

We are not asked to live the old natural life we were born in to. We are called to live this supernatural one that Jesus gave us. Which one are you living today? Are you still afflicted, under the dominion of that old man still. Discover today the power of His grace that enables you to rule and reign over all things right now? Which leads us perfectly into the next chapter.

CHAPTER 5

The Moment

The Divine Exchange

When the **MESSENGER** and **MESSAGE** match the **MISSION**, to restore the **MESS** in the chosen **MULTITUDE**, using God's eternal **METHOD**, **MODEL** and **MOTIVATION**, delivered at the **MOMENT** of His prompting, it brings supernatural **MULTIPLICATION** and the realignment of all things, into His likeness.

Use or Abuse

Everything created has a purpose. The creator created it with that purpose in mind. When created, the creator gave the created thing everything it needed to fulfill the desired purpose for why it was created. When the created item is used for what the creator intended it to be used for, then it accomplishes the task easily and successfully. When used for unintended purposes, the created thing ends up being abused and not fit for purpose. It often ends up broken because it was used for the wrong purpose, or it is not used at all because no-one actually understands its proper purpose. Not because anything was wrong with the design of the created item, but because it was not used for the purpose it was created for by the one who created it.

Let me say this clearly to you today and please stop a moment and fully register the depth of what I say to you dear reader. **The Church is not a religious institution!** It was never meant to be. It has become one due to man's desperate need to control everything.

When led to fulfill this wrong purpose, she ends up abusing, instead of using, the very people God added to her for her benefit. When trying to be what she was never created to be, the Church breaks what she was meant to mend, isolates what she was intended to reconcile, places burdens upon instead of lifting them from, turns inwards instead of outwards, focuses on the numbers attending rather than how many they are sending. She champions the judgement seat, rather than the mercy seat, where sinners discover how to appropriate His righteousness and grace to overcome all sin. Church platforms become the goal, when the Church was never designed to be a platform for anyone's gift.

Establishing The Culture Of The Kingdom

Jesus didn't come to preach a message, fill the earth with institutions and buildings called Churches, controlled by organizations who have strategies, goals, systems and programs. He came to demonstrate the life of Heaven on earth so we could see it.

When He spoke, touched, healed, loved and lived, it wasn't as if they sensed what it would be like in Heaven one day. They actually sensed what Heaven was like at that very moment in earth. Every part of Jesus was a taste of Heaven and the Kingdom of God in the here and now. He was offering everyone a new world culture to live in. He was so completely submitted to God's authority, that every word He spoke and every action He took, revealed the nature of God and His Kingdom.

He wasn't acting independent of Heaven's attention. He lived a life completely in alignment to Heaven and the Kingdom of God. He wasn't a signpost pointing the way to Heaven, He *was* the way of Heaven and the door to it. Heavens way was His way.

He was living to be Heaven's portal, an avenue for Heaven's light to travel through to disperse earths darkness. For three and a half years He realigned our thoughts, motives, attitudes, beliefs and desires by simply being Himself - the God of Life, more interested in healing than harming, justifying than judging, comforting and lifting, than condemning. He simply lived to fill His world with the glorious things of Heaven now, not in the future. The question is, do we? Do we want to?

What culture are we, His Church, demonstrating around the globe? In my humble opinion, I believe the Church is far from being like Heaven on Earth. There are glimpses of it, but not in many places it seems. Therefore, it is time for a major re-alignment with the Kingdom of God, deep within our 'root system' of understanding of who the Church is meant to be. The fruit of a tree is the result of the root system. If the fruit is bad, then change the root, not pick the fruit.

This unseen 'other world,' the prophets and preachers of the past proclaimed existed, literally stepped into this arena called earth, to reveal itself to us in the form of Jesus. Heaven and the Kingdom of

God, contrary to our thinking, was not trying to get us out of earth and into Heaven, but was pressing in upon the doorways of earth to bring Heaven and it's Kingdom life into it. After Adam and Eve sinned, they were put out of God's arena and the Father closed a door that had never before been closed (Gen 3:24).

When Jesus was born, the Father's shoulder began pressing against that door, closed for centuries, knowing that when His Son had finished His work, the door would be flung open wide for Him to once again permanently walk amongst us. Daily, such was God's delight and desire, that throughout the days of Jesus, Heaven pressed so hard upon the door, that it just could not be contained and it simply leaked through the door of His life and touched lives, displaying it's wonderful creative ability to realign everything to God's nature and life.

He is leaning upon the door right now because it's time for that life and glorious creative power to flood the earth yet again;

It's Preparation Day!

God does not live in 'time.' But He does step into it for a Moment and 'time' takes on the characteristics of eternity. In one of His 'moments' He turned everything around. He realigned everything. The death, burial and resurrection of Jesus, was the single, greatest 'Moment' creation had ever experienced.

As they buried Jesus, the disciples thought that everything they had hoped for was over. In their minds everything had changed. It had! Just not in the way they thought. They responded as people who thought everything was over. It seemed they hadn't grasped Jesus' words when He told them at the tomb of Lazarus *"I am the resurrection and the life."* (John 11:25) This life He talked about was a new kind of life. He demonstrated it to them. He was preparing them for what was to come. The Lord was about to reveal a new creation, a new species, a brand new kind of man! (2 Cor 5:17)

The day Jesus died was called 'Preparation Day.' (John 19:42) Jesus was preparing everyone, for the greatest event in creation's history. It is a tragedy when His Church camps at the message of the cross, which is the preparation for the real event, yet never fully experiences the real event itself, which is His resurrection life. Of course the cross is hugely important. A real central piece of our message. But the cross is not the end or the ultimate point of God's work through Christ. The resurrection and ascension of Christ is the pinnacle of our message. If we remain at the cross we have forgiveness for sin but no power to live in the life of the Spirit. We would have no authority over sin, death or the works of the Devil, because it is our being "seated in Christ far above every principality and power" (Eph 1:20-24) that empowers us to live in constant victory over all these things.

The One whom they laid in the tomb was the Lamb of God, who lovingly offered His life as a ransom for all sin and it's consequences. The price paid, the sacrifice accepted, the debt paid in full. The One who came out of the tomb was the Lord of all glory, the First and the Last, the Beginning and the End, who was and is and always will be. No longer confined by an earthly body, He is alive and well, living in His heavenly body doing things He had never done before. **What went into the tomb, is not what came out three days later.** Everything **had** changed.

The cross was the preparation for this new resurrection life of God, to fill the hearts of men. How tragic for believers in Christ to receive Him as their Savior, yet never live in the fulness of His Spirit and the resurrected life He offers us all. We have been enabled to live in the power of His new life, not just preach about it.

The Changing Faces of Jesus

If God mentions anything in His Word once, then it is important. If twice in a passage, then it is really important. If three times, then He is almost screaming at us to take note of the principle. If that is true, which I believe it is, then what is the Lord trying to do to us by saying something seven times in just a few verses of His Word? See how I have highlighted the words in the passage;

> *"After this, Joseph of Arimathea, being a disciple of Jesus, but secretly, for fear of the Jews, asked Pilate that he might **take away** the body of Jesus; and Pilate gave him permission. So he came and **took the body** of Jesus. And Nicodemus, who at first came to Jesus by night, also came, bringing a mixture of myrrh and aloes, about a hundred pounds. Then they **took the body** of Jesus, and bound it in strips of linen with the spices, as the custom of the Jews is to bury. Now in the place where He was crucified there was a garden, and in the garden a new tomb in which no one had yet been laid. So there they laid Jesus, because of the Jews' **Preparation Day**, for the tomb was nearby. Now on the first day of the week Mary Magdalene went to the tomb early, while it was still dark, and saw that the stone had been **taken away** from the tomb...............*
>
> *Then she ran and came to Simon Peter, and to the other disciple, whom Jesus loved, and said to them, "They have **taken away** the Lord out of the tomb, and we do not know where they have laid Him."..................*
>
> *Then they said to her, "Woman, why are you weeping?" She said to them, "Because they have **taken away** my Lord, and I do not know where they have laid Him." Now when she had said this, she turned around and saw Jesus standing there, and did not know that it was Jesus. Jesus said to her, "Woman, why are you weeping? Whom are you seeking?" She, supposing Him to be the gardener, said to Him, "Sir, if You have **carried Him away**, tell me where You have laid Him, and I will **take Him away**." Jesus said to her, "Mary!" She turned and said to Him, "Rabboni!" (which is to say, Teacher). Jesus said to her, "Do not cling to Me, for I have not yet ascended to My Father; but go to My brethren and say to them, 'I am ascending to My Father and your Father, and to My God and your God.'" Mary Magdalene came and told the disciples that she had seen the Lord, and that He had spoken these things to her. (John 19:38 - Ch 20:18)*

I remember reading this passage many years ago and seeing this pattern. It influenced me so deeply. How could it be there for all these years and no-one was preaching, or even mentioning it, when it was such an important issue to be grasped?

On that first day I was wondering why Mary, who had just been with Jesus three days before, was unable to recognize Him? I heard the Lord whisper into my spirit, "Would you like me to show you other occasions when the same thing happened?" Stunned by what I had heard, I responded affirming my desire to understand more fully. In a moment I felt led to turn to Mark 16:12;

> *"After that, He appeared in **another form** to two of them as they walked and went into the country."*

When I read *"another form"* I remember thinking what on earth could that mean? Out came my reference books to get to the real meaning of that phrase in the original Greek. Finally, I concluded I understood what it really meant. It meant exactly what the narrative boldly declares. He appeared in a different form! It was definitely Jesus, but not in a way He had ever been seen before. The Lord showed me more occasions when He did the same thing during that six week period between His resurrection and ascension.

Outside The Tomb

Mary arrives to find the tomb empty. Jesus speaks to her, but she doesn't recognize Him. She thinks Him to be the gardener. Why didn't Mary recognize Jesus, when she had seen Him just three days before? Had He changed in appearance? I believe He had. She fell at His feet to grasp hold of Him, but He would not be contained ever again. He vanished right in front of her eyes. He had never done this before.

Expect The Unexpected

"But their eyes were restrained so they did not know Him..........
then their eyes were opened and they knew Him and He vanished
from their sight" (Luke 24:16, 31)

The disciples in Emmaus, didn't recognize Him? Why not? They
knew Him well. They thought Him a stranger, until He took bread
and wine, and repeated the words they heard Him speak in the upper
room on the night Judas betrayed Him. They wondered how this man
could possibly know the very words Jesus used? In a moment, their
hearts were released from their dilemma so they could believe, and
when they believed they saw Him as He really was. Not how they had
always seen Him before. Now they saw Him for themselves in a way
they had never seen Him. They saw His eternal state. Immediately
He vanished from in front of them.

Hours earlier these guys were walking away from Jerusalem, and in
two opinions. Now they are running, not away from Jerusalem and all
the pain it represented, but back towards it. They were racing to tell
everyone the good news. No confusion now. Both of one opinion.....
Jesus is alive and He has changed. He had turned their lives around
in one moment. Yet, it is only just beginning for them!

You Can't Keep Him Out & You Can't Keep Him In

"saying The Lord is risen indeed and has appeared to Simon........
Now as they said these things, Jesus Himself stood in the midst of
them, and said to them, "Peace to you.: But they were terrified
and supposed they had seen a spirit. And he said to them, 'Why
are you troubled? And why do doubts arise in your hearts?' Behold
My hands and My feet, that it is I Myself.'" (Luke 24:34-39)

At this point, plenty of people have already seen Jesus in His
resurrected form. So why then is *'Peace to you'* His first words?
What do you think your reaction would be if one day, in a Church

service, the preacher suddenly walked through the wall and stood on the platform? I believe you would be utterly shocked and confused, with every paradigm of your thinking challenged in a moment. Instantly you would doubt that what you were seeing was true, because it is outside the box of everything you have ever experienced. There was total panic and confusion in the upper room.

But why didn't Mary announce it was Jesus and calm everyone down? Why are the two disciples from Emmaus silent, when they would, you think, be the ones to restore peace, recognizing that it was only Jesus in His new form? Could it possibly be that Jesus had changed His appearance once again, so none of them recognized Him? I believe He had.

> *"What went into the tomb, is not what came out three days later. Everything had changed."*

Just For One

"And after eight days His disciples were again inside, and Thomas with them. Jesus came, the doors being shut, and stood in the midst and said 'Peace to you!' Then He said to Thomas, reach your finger here, and look at My hands; and reach your hand here, and put it in My side. Do not be unbelieving, but believing."' (John 20:26-27)

Jesus appeared in the upper room on the first occasion when Thomas was not there. Have you ever turned up late to a meeting and everyone in the room starts saying "you should have been here - you missed it!" Then they recount to you the most amazing visitation of an angel or a miracle? Well, that's what happened to Thomas. Infuriating. He is grieving and confused. What should have encouraged him, was instead, hurting him even more. It would explain his response;

"I'll believe it when I see it with my own eyes." (Luke 20:25)

Thomas' belief system has been shattered by the events of the past few days. Thomas' heart was crying out to be brought to a place to believe again, like so many people today. Good people who have faithfully served the purposes of God for years, due to events along the journey, have, like Thomas, come to a place their hearts are so confused and shattered, that they need a personal visitation of Jesus to fix everything for them.

Eight days later Jesus walked through the wall a second time, just for Thomas! How incredibly sensitive and caring Jesus is for those He loves. His friend was broken, empty, grieving and confused. When he needed Jesus the most, He visited when he was not there. It made Thomas feel even worse.

It took just a few moments for Jesus to halt Thomas' sliding into a dark place. In one moment Thomas changes from being a doubter to a confessor, declaring *"my Lord and my God."* (v 28) The visitation turned Thomas' heart and life around. I believe, as the Lord brings us into this new move of His Spirit, He will do for His Church, what He did for Thomas!

Once again, Jesus' first words, when walking through the walls are, 'Peace to you,' followed by silence. Could it be that He has appeared looking differently again? I believe He did.

Have You Caught Any Fish?

""Children, have you any food? They answered Him 'No.'.........it is the Lord!" (John 21:5, 7)

"Jesus said to them, 'Come and eat breakfast,' yet none of them dared ask Him, 'Who are you?' - knowing it was the Lord." (John 21:12)

"And truly Jesus did many other signs in the presence of His disciples, which are not written in this book; but these are written that you may believe that Jesus is the Christ, the Son of God, and that believing you may have life in His Name." (John 20:30,31)

Whilst fishing unsuccessfully, Jesus calls out to them to cast their net the 'other side.' In other words, He wanted them to do it in a way they weren't. Simple! He just had to get them to turn around. When you turn around you get a completely different perspective and will see what you weren't seeing.

They just couldn't see that such a simple thing as doing it another way, would bring the harvest they were looking for. It would have been so easy for these experienced fishermen to have rejected this strangers suggestion, because, after all, they have been doing this as long as they could remember. Yes, that's true. But right now it is not working. And nor is Church, the way it is primarily done today. So Jesus wants us to see something 180% differently.

They turned around, cast the net and had a harvest. Only then does John declare *"It is the Lord."* (v 7) Excuse me? This is John, the apostle that was the closest to Jesus, and he doesn't recognize his best friend from just one hundred yards? (Ch 21:8) He only knew it was Jesus because of what He said and the miracle catch of fish.

When they get to the shore they are stunned. There on the beach is a fire with fish cooking for breakfast. Can you see the faces of the disciples when seeing the fish? How did Jesus get fish when they hadn't caught any all night? Simple! Jesus promised;

"If I be lifted up from the earth, I will draw all peoples to myself." (John 12:32)

He had been lifted up from the earth, on the cross and through the resurrection. It does not say in the original language that Jesus would draw all "peoples." That word was added into the narrative by the translators. It just says He would draw "all to Himself." There on the beach, shoals of fish had been drawn across the ocean by His presence, in order to fulfill His purpose. They swarmed around His feet. He needed some volunteers! They gladly offered up their lives to feed His brothers. This is why Jesus asked Peter;

"Do you love me more than these?" (John 21:15)

He wasn't asking Peter 'do you love me more than fishing?' These fish offered their lives just because Jesus asked it of them and Jesus was asking Peter if he loved Him the same way? As the disciples ate, it says;

"they knew it was Jesus, but no-one dared ask Him? (John 21:12)

He had changed His appearance again. They knew Him, not by natural eyesight, but through the things He said and did. He simply did not look like the Jesus they had known and trusted. He was making a demand on them to trust Him when eyes and logic do not understand.

The Appointed Mountain

"When they saw Him, they worshipped Him, but some doubted."
(Matt 28:17)

Matthew's account of the gathering at a mountain in Galilee, shows that Jesus kept changing His appearance each time they met Him. If He looked like He always had then they would not have doubted! In worshipping Him, it shows they deeply knew it to be Jesus. Yet, their eyes beheld the One they loved in another form.

The Wineskin Is Changing

Repeatedly in the passage from John's Gospel, I highlighted the words that refer to Jesus' body being 'taken away.' These few verses reveal the same pattern;

> *"The first man Adam became a living being." The last Adam became a life giving spirit. **However, the spiritual is not first, but the natural, and afterward the spiritual.** The first man was of the earth, made of dust; the second man is the Lord from Heaven. As was the man of dust, so also are those who are made of dust; **and as is the heavenly Man, so also are those who are heavenly.** And as we have borne the image of the man of dust, we shall also bear the image of the heavenly man." (1 Cor 15:45-49)*

> *"He **takes away** the first that He may establish the second." (Heb 10:9)*

Hebrews shows the pattern that God took away the Ark of the Covenant, the Tabernacles, the sacrificial offerings, Levitical priesthood, the Old Covenant, and finally, in AD70 the Temple and it's system was totally demolished. They were all the earthly copies and shadows (Col 2:17; Heb 8:5; Heb 10:1) pointing to Jesus, the heavenly, spiritual, better and true manifestation of them all. So, the old was removed, their purpose accomplished.

His earthly body was removed in order for us to see and receive, the new heavenly one. He did not leave us a choice to live in both the old and the new (Col 2:14). By removing the old, He is demanding we live in the new. This pivotal moment challenged the apostles, as it does us. They had a choice to live either the life of the natural Adam and the flesh, or by faith, release this new creation, the new man, who bares the image and nature of the heavenly Christ. One viewing everything from the natural, earthly and limited perspective, the other, from the heavenly vantage point of being seated, in Christ, the place of dominion and no limitations.

What Went In Did Not Come Out!

"Therefore, from now on, we regard no one according to the flesh. Even though we have known Christ according to the flesh, yet now we know Him thus no longer. Therefore, if anyone is in Christ, he is a new creation; old things have passed away; behold, all things have become new." (2 Cor 5:16-17)

This whole chapter has been written to show, you have a choice to make. Do you live in the likeness of the old man or the new man, the old way or God's new way?
Our old sinful nature was taken away in Christ. You were given this new nature of God which is perfect, victorious and can realign everything back to the Father.

Our choice today, is to either live from our external fleshly nature, which is crucified with Christ, or believe God's Word and live in the fullness of this new heavenly Christ-Life, dwelling within us. A life of unlimited grace, peace, joy and victory over all the works of the Devil. Take your seat. The ride is already paid for!

A PROPHETIC WORD FOR THE MOMENT

In January 2011 whilst I approached the platform to minister in Manchester, UK, the Holy Spirit spoke a prophetic revelation into my spirit. Within seconds my message had changed. As I shared this word of revelation, so the group of people in the room exploded into praise, rejoicing, shouting ecstatically.

As I took the final steps towards the microphone, so the Holy Spirit had asked me, "son, where are you coming from and where are you going?" I knew He wasn't referring to the geographical when asking. I knew He was referring to the calendar date. I swiftly replied "I have just left 2010, and have just entered 2011 and on my way to 2012." He needed to say no more because I knew the implication immediately. You see, when I attended the Bible College of Wales, one of my mentors explained that the purpose of his ministry to me, whilst in the college, wasn't to teach me Bible knowledge, but to expose to me the pattern of God through principles.
Intrigued, I asked him to explain. He replied that many in the Church seemed to not realize the importance God places on numbers in the Bible. Then he also shared with me that each number had a significance. Such as number 4 meant balance, five was the number of Grace. Over the years since that conversation I have come to discover the meanings of many numbers in the Bible, and it was all those things that were flooding my spirit as I walked to the platform that evening.

The number ten represents the full giving of the Word of God, represented by the Ten Commandments. The number Twelve represents the full expression of God's government in the earth, seen when looking at Jacob's twelve sons, Israel's twelve tribes and the twelve disciples and apostles that Jesus chose to establish His Church foundations. But it was the year 2011 and the number eleven represents man's rebellion, as seen in the account of the Tower of Babel (Gen 11) and the rebellion of Judas to God's way and will. I quickly asked the Lord "Are you telling me that there is going to be a season of rebellion in the Church?" The reply was both relieving and shocking at the same time. He unfolded to me that the Church had received a long season of teaching from the Word over the past fifty to sixty years and how the Church had Bibles in every conceivable language and style. The Bible was available on Audio CD, DVD's of messages in their millions, Christian bookshops in cities all over the world, bookstores with online availability of every Christian book written on every conceivable subject. We have Churches everywhere, Church on Radio, TV and all day and night on the internet and have had nonstop conferences trying to equip the Church. We had received abundant teaching on His Word for a purpose.He informed me that we were heading for a season where the powerful manifestation of God's government was going to flow into the earth.

"All rebellion is not evil."

In between the season of the giving of the Word (2010) and the manifestation of His government (2012), stood a season of rebellion (2011). Clearly and loudly into my spirit came an almost audible voice affirming me to tell His people everywhere, that it was a season of godly rebellion and uprising in the earth. With authority He told me to tell His people, to rebel against anyone and anything that tried to prevent them from being all He had created them to be and do. I also knew that much of what His people needed to rebel out of, was the religious system of control mechanisms used in so many

Churches. I also knew, this would be a season that would shake the Church institutions and that leaders would label it 'rebellion.' But all rebellion is not evil. There is also a godly rebellion when people come out from under dictatorship, or abusive controlling structures in order to do what God's Word says.

First The Natural, Then The Spiritual

"However, the spiritual is not first, but the natural, and afterward the spiritual." (1Cor 15:46)

That evening after declaring this prophetic word in Manchester, I turned on the news channel and saw the pictures of the broadcasts of the uprisings in North Africa, which spread across to the Middle East and even into the Far East. As I watched the news of this sudden uprising, so I heard the Father's voice a second time. He spoke the words of 1Cor 15:46 to me, telling me that what I was watching was happening in the earth because everything had changed in the heavenlies and it was a prophetic sign that the Church was going to embrace a sudden wave of people breaking out of an old wineskin. There would be hostility as people broke free of religion, rules and regulations into the liberty of the Holy Spirit, to become part of the greatest move of God the earth has ever seen, bringing spiritual climate change everywhere. (It is interesting that climate change is such a big issue at this moment!).

Can you sense this change coming? Are you ready for it? Hold on then, because it's about to start a holy revolution within the Church.

CHAPTER 6

The Messeger

The Doorkeeper Of The Treasury

When the **MESSENGER** and **MESSAGE** match the **MISSION**, to restore the **MESS** in the chosen **MULTITUDE**, using God's eternal **METHOD**, **MODEL** and **MOTIVATION**, delivered at the **MOMENT** of His prompting, it brings supernatural **MULTIPLICATION** and the realignment of all things, into His likeness.

The Bible begins in an earthly garden (Gen 2:8) and ends in a heavenly one (Rev 22:1). Both center around a tree. The opening chapters reveal the natural Adam (man) and the closing ones with a supernatural 2nd Adam (Jesus and His Bride, the Body of Christ). In the middle of the Bible, like a caterpillar, the one is transformed into the other at a tree (the cross), in a garden (the tomb). The old Adam dies, is removed and a new creation, the 2nd Adam bursts out of the tomb displaying the unfathomable, uncontainable, un-limitable life of God, which every believer was to receive and enjoy.

If we do not grasp the enormity of this truth, then the Church will always operate out of the old carnal ability and nature of the 1st Adam. But the true Church is not an earthly institution, but is a Heaven birthed organism. The true Church operates in 'Zoe life,' which is the life of God. It is His life, in all it's fullness, now living and abiding in the hearts of every follower of Christ. Why, when we see how little this outer earthly man can do, in comparison to what the Christ-life within us can do, would we continue for one more day, working, operating, out of the old adamic, flesh man? Flesh reproduces more flesh. The Spirit reproduces more of the life of the Spirit. Earthly produces earthly, whilst Heavenly produces Heavenly.

The very first verses in the Bible reveal a principle and pattern of all life. Life produces life after it's own likeness (Gen1:11). Within all of creation, everything that has life follows this principle. The DNA it contains reproduces after it's own likeness. The Church must awaken to the reality that it has been given the Father's DNA. We are birthed by Him, to be like Him. The way we live, speak and think, reveals which DNA is reproducing. The 1st or 2nd Adam? The heavenly or earthly nature? DNA multiplies, fashioning around itself attributes, abilities and everything it needs, to live life to its fulness. This life of God is within every follower of Christ.

The offer of this transfer, was purchased for us by the death of Jesus and given to us through His grace. For us to walk in the fullness of all he purchased and paid for, then we have to allow His grace to bring us to the death of our efforts, to be who He wants us to be and do what He wants us to do. We must allow His grace to change us and outwork itself in and through us. Grace is God's free gift to us because of Jesus. It is free, but not cheap! It costs the death of the 1st Adam, the body of Jesus. Our cost is to reckon this same man is dead and the 2nd Adam is alive and well in us.

> *"Therefore, from now on, we regard **no one according to the flesh**. Even though we **have known Christ** according to the flesh, yet now **we know Him thus no longer**. Therefore, if anyone is in Christ, he is a new creation; **old things have passed away; behold, all things have become new**." (2Cor 5:16-17).*

We are commanded to not focus on the 'fleshly' man. Not you, other believers, or Jesus, in this way. Why? Because if you are "in Christ," then your 'new man' has the nature of the resurrected Christ, not the one who went to the cross.

Jesus lived and operated after the cross and His death, differently than He did before it. The life He lived before His death was limited to the natural body of the 1st Adam. But after His resurrection His new body knew no such limitations. It kept changing. No walls kept Him in or out. He appeared and disappeared. This miraculous transformation speaks of ours. He purchased it for us to live it, not just preach or produce films about it.

It's The End of Me!

This work of His grace will bring us to a place of complete trust in His work and an end to trusting in our own strengths and abilities to fulfill the will of God. The kingdom of man is upside down to the Kingdom of God. His strength is revealed in our weakness. His ability flows when we have none left. Mans world depends on individual might and money. God's world depends upon the Spirit and the Word and none of me. It's an upside down, inside out paradigm shift. My obedience means more to Him than my talent. Obedience enables His ability to flow. I can have the greatest talent in the world and it can move the soul and influence man. But He influences the heavenlies, earth and all of creation when I obey. Jesus was spat upon, ridiculed and rejected by all men and man closed the door of a tomb on Him. But His willingness to remain in the place of obedience upon a cross, even to death, opened wide Heavens portal and the resources of God poured out.

Jesus lived to be Heaven's doorkeeper, allowing God's Spirit to flow, bringing to earth all that lay upon Heaven's table. The world was changed for the worse by the nature of the 1st Adam. It will be changed and brought back into alignment with God by the nature of the 2nd Adam. When the Church truly accepts the heavenly exchange on offer, the doors of His treasury will fling wide open.

The Doorkeepers of God's Treasury

"For the LORD God had not caused it to rain on the earth, and there was no man to till the ground; but a mist went up from the earth and watered the whole face of the ground." (Gen 2:5-6)

Which is better? For you to be able to open the door of God's treasury, or to be an earthly king and open the door of yours? Whose treasury is greater?

The rain, the unseen 'treasure' of God, was available and in place, but could not flow into the earth, until God formed a man. Adam was fashioned, placed by God in the garden and given an assignment. He was fashioned and gifted with abilities that would enable him to do the task with ease.

He was placed on the east side of the garden (v 8) to work and protect it (Gen 1:27-28; Ch 2:5). He was to control what came in and what didn't come in, to the garden. No fancy job or title, just a simple door opener, a porter. The important thing is not the doorkeeper, or their title, but the one who walks through the door when opened!

Adam - God's First Portal

Knowing who you are to **be** precedes you doing what you're meant to **do**. I don't believe the narrative of Genesis is meant to make us focus on Adam's work, but upon **who** he is meant to be in the garden. The revelation of **who** he was meant to be, in His relationship with God, would release God's grace for him to fulfill God's assignment. Jesus confirmed this when at the well in John 4;

"But the hour is coming, and now is, when the true worshipers will worship the Father in spirit and truth; for the Father is seeking such to worship Him." (John 4:23)

The oldest Biblical word for worship means 'intimacy.' The Father 'seeks' intimacy with man. You can't have intimacy with a system, a theology or tradition. You have it with a real person. It is the condition of your heart towards the other person. Adam's first responsibility was to **be** the person God fashioned him to be, which was a worshipper. The assigned task (what he had to **do**), was as a gatekeeper and porter. **Never confuse the difference between your purpose and your function!** Your purpose in life is to be a 'son' of God, which depicts your relationship and intimacy with the Father. Your function is to be a gatekeeper, a portal, for His Kingdom. Doing what He has called you to do places you in the correct environment for His latent ability within you to flow through you, via the ministry He has called you to do, using the gifts He has distributed in you. But never forget, the 'doing' flows out of the 'being.' Worship opens the gates of Heaven so His Kingship can flow into the earth. The worshipper, through their intimacy, opens the gates so the King can flow in to the earth.

Adam is the gateway for the creative order and ability of Heaven, to flow into the earth. But this is entirely dependent upon Adam staying in his assigned place of being an intimate worshipper of the Father. The relationship with Father preceded his responsibility to Eve and the rest of the earth. God could fashion Adam, but only Adam could determine if he would be a worshipper. It was his free-will choice. It is the same for us. You can attend meetings, join in with Church activities, fully involved with the programs of the Church, yet never discover true intimacy with the Father and know the release of His power that brings everything in your world into alignment with Him.

Judah - The Worshippers & Warriors

The tribe of Judah were always camped at the entrance of the Tabernacle of worship (Num 2:3). They were the guardians and doorkeepers of the presence of God in the camp and throughout Israel's history. They led Israel into battle. They camped outside the door of the Tabernacle. The word 'Judah' comes from the Hebrew word 'Yadah,' which means to stretch out your hands in praise. Judah, the warrior (Jud 20:18), is also the worshipper.

One worshipper, who worships in spirit and in truth, provides God the open door and gateway, for His Kingdom to fill the earth, bringing all things that are out of alignment back into alignment to His Word and will.

It was in Eden that Adam walked with God daily (Gen 3:8). It was an environment so perfectly fashioned that both God and man were at 'home' in it. Eden was the place of perfect alignment. Adam being correctly aligned to God, was his assigned place and created an atmosphere so powerful that the river of God flowed out of that place of intimacy and watered the whole earth, therefore releasing the latent potential of every seed planted anywhere. Adam being correctly aligned to his assignment was essential for the development of God's purposes and plans in the earth. This pattern is God's eternal pattern for us, His Church.

'Eden' means 'home.' A house speaks of a building. A home speaks of the family and atmosphere within it. The Church building is not the House or home of God. He does NOT dwell in a man-made buildings. The born again believers, individually and collectively, are the 'home' and 'house' of God forever. The first picture in the Bible is God in a place called 'home.' He was at 'home' with Adam. Then, if this is what was lost through Adam's sin, it is what has been given back to us in and through Christ. Therefore, let us concentrate our focus to restore our personal and collective intimacy with the Father, until it is evident to all He is at home with us all over again.

"You can't have intimacy with a system, a theology or tradition.
You have it with a real person."

The Oldest Trick - Distraction

One minute the picture in Genesis is of God's perfect order, the next everything has gone wrong. The serpent was in the tree and had caused Adam and Eve to disobey God. What could have happened? The serpent, had no power over Adam to stop him. God's hand was upon his life. The serpent, Lucifer, therefore used a simple distraction and deception to get get Adam to step out of his assigned place and accept the lie as the truth. Lucifer's tactic's have never changed to this day.

The original language of Hebrew, the Bible speaks of Adam having an assignment from God to guard and protect. It is as though on the East side of the garden there was a gate. Adam's role was to stay at the gate and guard what came into the garden. Where do we find him? He is in the middle of the garden, with his wife, tricked into taking fruit from a serpent. How did the serpent get in? It seems from the narrative that first the serpent attracted Eve, who then persuaded her husband to come and eat of the fruit of the tree. Adam was lured from his assignment by his wife. Now, before you send any letters of hostility to me for saying this and feeling I am being sexist, which I honestly am not, let me explain.

Eve simply represents someone or something close to Adam, that Lucifer used to distract him from trusting the Father. The Father had told them to never eat of this tree. To now find Adam and Eve eating the fruit from the tree, means they did not trust God's word and motive to be absolutely the truth and trustworthy.

Eve, the one fashioned of God to be Adam's helper, has become the leader in the relationship. She is the one who first believes the serpent and takes the fruit (Gen 3:1-6). She stepped out of her God-given place and assignment and was then one who then persuaded her husband to do likewise. The serpent's words convinced Eve, who then convinced Adam to believe the serpent instead of the Father.

The moment they believed the doubt, their relationship with the Father distanced, for it was no longer on the basis of trust and perfect love for each other. The doubts within them made them believe they could not ultimately trust God's motive and words, therefore needed to make the decisions themselves. The serpent persuaded them both, through doubt, to leave their assignment of being lovers of God above all people, including themselves and instead, trust their own judgement and wisdom above the Fathers. They placed themselves as No1 in their own eyes. This was Lucifer's same downfall in heaven (Isa 14:12-14).

When Adam and Eve stepped out of alignment in their relationship with the Father, they also lost their ability to fulfill and keep their God given place of assignment as the door-keepers to all of God's provisions for the earth and it's environment.

The point I am trying to make is that it is not bad things that distract us from our role in life, but often good things. It's great we do good things as Christians, but are they the same as doing the God assigned things? If not, then realignment needs to happen in our lives. Church life is filled with activities and responsibilities. But if those 'good' things prevent us from doing the 'God' things, then we are being distracted, deceived, pulled out of position and the provisions of God dry up and the river cannot flow.

We are to bear fruit, not just foliage (activity)!

*"By this My Father is glorified, that you bear much **fruit**"*
(John 15:8)
*"You did not choose Me, but I chose you and appointed you that
you should go and bear **fruit**; and that your **fruit** should remain."*
(John 15:16)

It seems to me that the structure of Church life so often established today, focuses more on the required attendance to meetings, than a person fulfilling God's will and being fruitful. Adam and Eve's role was to be guardians in the 'home' and place of intimacy. They were to guard the place of intimacy with the Father, which was the bedrock of intimacy with one another. God intended this place of intimacy to be the foundation for all family life. Being lovers of God, keeping Him in the highest place in their hearts, was their highest place of assignment. Their relationship with one another was dependent upon this one thing. All fruitfulness in life was to flow from being faithful in their relationship with Father. Fruitfulness is not activated, or evidenced, by activities, but by intimacy. The activities are the external evidence of the intimacy we have with the Father and one another. The activity cannot take priority over intimacy in any relationship. The goal is always intimacy and the activity follows afterwards. The fruit is the evidence of the root abiding in it's assigned placed, even though it is unseen to the naked eye.

The great commission (to make disciples of all nations) must never take precedence over the great commandment (to love God with all of your heart). It is a horrible reality to realize that you can spend your life doing missions and good works, yet never truly experience intimacy with the Father. Working for Him is no replacement for our worship of Him. This to me is the very key to why so much of the world is still unreached with His gospel, even though huge amounts of finances are poured into mission projects around the world. It is not that missions and world evangelization is not hugely important. Of course it is. But our fruitfulness in our works and activities is conditional upon our personal relationship with Him. Our love for one another is simply the overflow of our love for Him. We cannot give that which we have not received first from Him (1 Jn 4:19). We love because He loved us first. Our outworking of His love is a direct result of the in-working of it. If it is not His loving personal relationship with you, that causes you to do works for Him, then what is? The work we do must also be done flowing from the same motive He does everything in the earth;

*"God so **loved** the world, that He gave His only Son." (Jn 3:16)*

When I allow His love for me to captivate me, it will allow His love to flow through me to this world. Then they will not hear a message about His love for them, they will experience it first-hand. After-all, I am just the branch that the life of the vine (Jesus) passes through because it is abiding in right alignment with Him.

This is simple, yes? Then why have we made it so complicated and burdensome for so many? We need a simple realignment in the understanding, focus and emphasis of Church life that allows people to flourish, flow and be fruitful in their walk with God. It begins with focusing on our intimacy with God at home first.

Broken Internal Relationship Leads To External Religion?

From Genesis to Revelation the pattern of God seems quite simple. He begins the restoration of all things by re-establishing the place of intimacy with mankind. From the moment Adam sins, we see our Father stepping into the moment. Then there is the death of an innocent being, the shedding of it's blood and the covering of man (Gen 3:21). It was earth's first altar. Adam had never known an external place of worship with a physical altar. His heart and his life had always been the altar and place of worship. What had been on the inside of Adam, was now going to take place on the outside. But there was prophesied at that very moment, One called the Seed (Gen 3:15), would come and rectify it all and restore the place of worship back into the heart of every worshipper.

When Christ came, He paid for all sin and it's consequences. He destroyed the power of sin in a believers life and imputed into each born again believer His righteousness. He gave them a new heart (Jer 24:7). He restored the heart of every follower back into His sanctuary and home. He absolutely destroyed the necessity of an external altar, sacrifice or location of worship. In one moment He demolished the religious system. There was no need for a Temple, or it's systems. His Temple was the body of believers who embraced Him as Savior and Lord.

Throughout the ages, the Church has fallen back into focussing the attention on everything being earthly and external. They have rebuilt the buildings, the altars, the garments, the structures, all removed in Christ. The focus and emphasis, so much today, upon the worship in a building being of greater importance, than in our hearts and home. The 'system' has cast out the way God wants it done and has returned to what God destroyed through His Son. We wonder why things aren't working the way the New Testament shows they can.

Each new move of God in history, has come to remove us from the 'religious' enclave and formats of Church and restore us back to personal intimacy with God, which is true 'worship.' History also records the tragic truth, that the institutionalized Church system, persecuted these 'apostles' of God who come to restore the Church to its true foundations and align it back to Christ the Chief cornerstone. It's happening again! The apostles of truth are rising with a message of realignment. Watch the sparks fly!

Personal intimacy with God in the home, is the epicenter and catalyst for every move of God. It leads to revival. If one worshipper can move God to pour out a reviving spirit across a nation, then what on earth will happen if we could raise a whole generation of worshippers? What if this assigned place was taken up by households in a city or region?

The Holy Spirit is drawing the whole Church into this alignment and that is why we will see the greatest outpouring of the Holy Spirit known to man and creative miracles will be normal? Many have prophesied that this next move of God will not be through world renowned individual preachers, but by a multitude of unknowns. I too believe this. I believe it will cause believers to reject, on mass, this old 'carcass' of religiosity and return to the place of true intimacy with God and one another. The result will be the overflow of His life, grace and power.

Be careful. Do not misunderstand what I am saying. I am not advocating christians independently doing their 'own thing.' Absolutely not! I am an avid believer the Church needs to gather together and work together. I just do not believe it has to be in a weekly format, in a specific location, in a certain sort of building called 'Church, at a special time. I believe this new season will reveal a new type of believer, one who is more Kingdom mission focused, than 'stream' orientated. Streams are great, rivers are better, the ocean even greater.
I believe this move of God will utterly remove the worries of the barriers of theology and styles of Church, as Christians gather together from across the divides, to worship, work and witness together, as one Body, to see His Mission fulfilled. His Kingdom can only be displayed in the world, to the measure the Church displays His Kingdom to one another. There may be many streams and denominations, but only one Kingdom.

Bethel - The Portal of God

"Then Jacob awoke from his sleep and said, 'surely the Lord is in this place, and I did not know it.' And he was afraid and said 'How awesome is this place! This is none other than the house of God and this is the gate of Heaven." (Gen 28:16,17)

The Church is in the earth to be the portal of God. It's sole purpose is to be the gate of Heaven. Jesus was the place where Heaven's supernatural life flowed out, restoring earth into heaven's image. We have been made in His image and for this same purpose.

In Genesis 28:10-22 we find the account of Jacob, when traveling through a wilderness, stopped and made camp because it was dark. This is God's covenant man. Yet we find him wandering, in the dark, in a barren climate, ending up pitching camp. So many in the Church are presently experiencing the same thing. They are going through the motions, as if wandering in circles, living as if in the dark, not knowing what God seems to be doing in the earth. They are faithful, but unfruitful.

The first two chapters of Genesis shows clearly that EVERYTHING God makes is fruitful. The Church has now got to the place where we are spending a fortune on Church Growth conferences, materials, buildings, media equipment, internet, radio and television ministry to make the Church grow. Still it isn't. We have 'transfer' from one congregation to another, but not much genuine growth.

The question is not how can we make the Church grow but what stops it? Could it be we, like Adam, have become deceived and distracted from purpose?

Leaving our assigned place of intimacy with the Father causes us to end up in the same place as Adam, wearing the foliage but bearing no fruit (Gen 3:7). The fruit is the outside manifestation of the inward life. You are born of God. His life abides in you for a purpose. He desires it to flow through you, to restore to the earth His image and likeness. Heaven in earth through every believer is the mandate!

Jacob lay down and dreamt. His ability to dream and to see into the unseen had not been lost, it had never truly been 'awakened.' So God creates a perfect environment to kick-start Jacobs dormant gifting. That is what the Lord is asking you to do right now. Allow Him to bring you to a place to begin to dream again and 'see' into the unseen and untapped resources of God waiting to flow into this life through you.

As Jacob slept, he dreams of Heaven's door opening and he wakes up! Thank God this is also happening all over the world. God's people are waking up to their purpose and calling. This world will not be changed by mega-churches, but by the waking up of God's sleeping giant, the priesthood of all believers.

Jacob is shocked at the event and establishes an altar and worships God, naming this place of supernatural manifestation as 'Bethel,' which means 'House or home of God.' Wow, the Home of God is the gate, the doorway, the portal between Heaven and earth and is testified as being the place of supernatural manifestations flowing into the earth. A place of signs and wonders. A place of intimacy with God and one another. If you are born again, then this is pointing to you, the dwelling, abiding place of God.

In both David's Tabernacle and Solomon's Temple, the musicians and singers (worshippers), also had the role of being the doorkeepers (Ps 84:10; 1 Chron 26:1). Here again is the connection to worshippers being the ones who can open the doors for the King to flow in and out. Our nations don't just need great preaching and teaching, they need the whole body of Christ to rise up into the revelation that each Christian can become that doorkeeper of God's Treasury.

Bethel is the 'home' of God, not hotel of God. The difference being that one is visited and the other lived in. God doesn't desire to visit meetings. He desires to take up residence in the earth. If He saves, heals and delivers when He visits, what on earth will He do when He resides!

It is time dear friend, to open the doors of His treasury within you. It is time to live the lifestyle of continual worship from the place of intimacy with the Father (Acts 2:4;1Cor 12:10; 14:15; Jude v 20). You have been fashioned for this very Moment.

CHAPTER 7

The Message

The Gospel of His Grace

When the **MESSENGER** and **MESSAGE** match the **MISSION**, to restore the **MESS** in the chosen **MULTITUDE**, using God's eternal **METHOD**, **MODEL** and **MOTIVATION**, delivered at the **MOMENT** of His prompting, it brings supernatural **MULTIPLICATION** and the realignment of all things, into His likeness.

*"In the beginning was the Word, and the Word was with God, and the Word was God..................And the Word became flesh and dwelt among us, and we beheld His glory, the glory as of the only begotten of the Father, **full of grace** and truth." (John 1:1, 14)*

John's opening words are explosive, unrestrained, emphatic and clear. He declares   Jesus the Messenger, His Message and Ministry is not only the Word of God, but that He **was** and is God. Everything else he writes, is placed upon this foundational understanding.

He writes the first seventeen verses of his gospel instructing us that the Word, who is Jesus, was there at the beginning and was the Creator of all things. He tells us the Word is Life and the Light, and darkness could not comprehend (grasp, understand, hold, possess) it. He then reveals the Word of God, Jesus Christ, was full of grace and truth.

The Messenger is the Message!

The Messenger, His Message and Ministry, were one and the same, from beginning to end. His message has **always** been full of grace and truth, because He **is** grace and truth. If He is grace, then He can never **not be** grace. Grace is not a theology but a person called Jesus. To reject His grace is to reject who Jesus is.

Grace is our Savior, deliverer, healer and preserver, who swapped places with us, took on our sinful nature and the punishment of all our sin. When we turn from our sin into faith in Christ, it is Grace who imputes into us His glorious life, righteousness and perfection. So, to reject grace is to reject all of this and try to save yourself from the clutches of sin and death, overcome all the consequences of sin by your own ability and stand in your own righteousness hoping you've done enough to claim a place in Heaven for eternity. I know which one is the best deal! I'll chose grace any day! Jesus said;

*"I **am** the way, the truth and the life" (Jn 14:6)*
*"I **am** the Light" (Jn 8:12)*
*"I **am** the resurrection." (Jn 11:25)*

*"I **am** the bread of life." (Jn 6:35, 41)*

Jesus didn't just preach a message. He was the message. He was the message, the Word of God, lived out in it's entirety for all to see and experience, not just hear. I appreciate we cannot be all that He is, because He is the Son of God. My point is that He was what He preached. Then so must we desire to be the same. We must take on the likeness of the message He has given us to bring to the nations. We can believe and preach the theological message of Grace with such clarity, yet still live a life that clearly reveals we are still in bondage trying to live up to the law and telling others to do the same.

Information or Impartation?

The New Testament reveals the Messenger and the Message are to be one and the same. A message that is purely a theological standpoint, something we have been taught along the way, which has not been fully worked into our own lifestyle, will have little influence on others, because it has not influenced us personally. We will simply preach information instead of bringing impartation. Information is a communication of mental ascent, whilst impartation flows out of the true revelation coming directly from the throne of God, rising up from our spirit within us. It does not come from our head, it comes to and from our spirit. It is spirit to spirit communication, from God the Spirit to our spirit. True revelation will take on appearance in the flesh, just as Jesus, the Seed of God, came from Heaven and took on the likeness of man in the flesh. My friend understand clearly that Jesus took on the nature of man, that man may take on the nature of God. Jesus took on the image of unrighteous man, that unrighteous man might take on the righteous image of God. This is not theory until we get to Heaven one day. Grace is not a characteristic of God that ignores, or looks away, from our times of sin, as if it's ok to sin because He has grace towards us. That characteristic is the mercy of God. Grace is God's ability that can work within you to set you free from sin that continually harasses and controls you. It is His power to change you into His likeness, even here on earth. Grace changes your heart and out of your heart flows your life.

The opposite characteristics of grace and truth, are law and deception. People can preach whatever they want, but if it is not firmly founded on the revelation that God's message is grace, then what is being preached is the re-enforcement of the law. Those that preach external works make us acceptable to God, are preaching that legalism is the way to salvation and are not understanding they are rejecting the free gift of salvation given through Christ. They are replacing His free gift of righteousness, with a legalistic mechanism of laws to earn the blessings of God, which can **never** be responded to by God. I am not saved and made acceptably righteous by the good 'christian' works that I perform. I am not righteous because I do not drink alcohol, smoke cigarettes, wear piercings through my nose or eyebrows and refuse to have a tattoo. I am not being a good christian because I go to meetings, tithe, faithfully serve in a church family. All these things are pure choice of your personal preference or conscience. They are all external and cannot make an unrighteous person righteous in the eyes of God. They may be righteous in the eyes of christians or a denomination, but not in the sight of God. There is only one way we gain acceptance to the Father. It is through the imputed righteousness of His Son when I turn away from living without Him and turn towards Him as my Lord and Savior. I then work out my salvation to live to please Him, not to be acceptable to Him.

The law was perfect and from God. But it could not change anyone. It was perfect, just like the One who wrote it with His finger. It was, in a sense, bad news to people, because it continually reminded everyone of their sin and imperfection and that it was impossible to change and be righteous enough for Heaven. That was the very purpose God gave it to the people. It was to show them that they could **never** live perfectly enough to obtain all the blessings of God. It was the tutor (Gal 3:24-25), the teacher, that would lead everyone to understand this truth and accept His free gift of grace in Christ. What no-one could do for themselves, He did on our behalf. He took on our curse of sin and death and all it's consequences, and offered to all mankind His righteousness and resurrection life, with all it's benefits, if we just accept Christ as Lord and Savior.

I am sorry if I offend anyone, but I am tired of such preaching that says I must tithe to open the windows of Heaven and receive the blessings of God. This is just not true. The Old Covenant was fulfilled and wiped out by the blood of Jesus, at the cross (Col 2:14). If you have received the free gift of salvation in Jesus Christ, then you have entered into the New Covenant with God, based upon His grace, not your works.

Because of Jesus the window of Heaven is wide open towards you. You do **not** get blessed because you tithe. You tithe because you have **been** blessed with every blessing in Christ. We need to stop asking Him to bless us. **He has**, with everything He is and all He possesses. He cannot bless us any more. We need to ask Him to help us comprehend the enormity of His grace, so that it can do it's full work in and through us.

His Grace Is The Good News!

The word gospel means 'good news.' If Christianity is all about living under the law, which I cannot fulfill and therefore cannot receive the blessings it promises, then how is that 'good news?' The good news is that Jesus Christ came, perfectly fulfilled every bit of the law, on my behalf, and gave me all the blessings it promised, as a free gift. If I still have to earn it from God, then it is not a free gift is it? If I still have to live up to some standard to trigger the flow of blessing, then why did Jesus die for me? What was the point? Either He did it for me, or I have to do it for myself. It can't be both. The good news is that I don't have to earn it at all. I just receive all of its blessings and abundance through accepting Jesus as my Savior and Lord. Now **that's** good news!

God is grace. He has always been grace. 'Let there be light' were words of grace, not law. Creation is founded upon and held together, by His Word of grace (Heb 1:3). You are saved by grace (Eph 2:8). You were redeemed, forgiven of every sin, made acceptable to God, received His wisdom and obtained His inheritance, by His gift of grace (Eph 1:6-11). Everything He is and has is ours through His grace, not based upon works at all (Rom 11:6).

If you are in grace, then you are no longer under law(Rom 6:14). The Old Covenant was based on the law, the New Covenant upon His grace. You cannot have one foot in each covenant. But sadly, this is what is so often preached and believed in Churches around the world.

If you are under any part of the law, then you remain under the curse that was removed in Christ (Gal 3:10-14). The curse is revealed in that no matter how good you try to be, you will miss the mark of perfection. Guilt will then condemn you and declare to you that you cannot please God. But if under grace, then sin has no hold on you at all, because His forgiveness has removed your sin and has made you acceptable in the beloved (Eph 1:6).

Grace was so fundamentally important to Paul, that he begins and ends every one of his letters with a salutation of grace. God's work begins and ends with grace. In Romans 16:24 and 1 Corinthians 1:3 he declares *"grace was given to all."* He could not possibly declare this, unless he knew everyone's salvation was by grace.

His ministry of laying foundations, as a wise master builder, was given to him by God's grace (1Cor 3:10). His understanding is that the very foundations of all God is saying and doing through the gospel, is founded upon His grace.

In 2Cor 8:9 he exhorts us all to **know** the grace of the Lord Jesus Christ. He reveals this grace of God **abounds** towards you (2 Cor 9:8), that you are filled with **exceeding** grace of God (2Cor 9:14). He even warns that there are preachers who **pervert** (turn around) the gospel of grace (Gal 1:7) and he declares those who turn back from the gospel of grace and embrace another gospel (the law) as being 'foolish' and 'bewitched,' (Gal 1:6).

The word 'estranged' is often used when describing the breakdown in a marriage. It simply means 'separated, distanced, removed from, or cold hearted towards the one you were once in love with.' Paul uses this word to describe what happens when someone turns away from living by grace and returns to living under the law (Gal 5:4). Legalism brings a coldness and distance between you and God. That's what it was like before you got saved! You were alienated from God (Eph 4:18/Col 1:21). But when you received Christ, you received grace and were reconciled to Him. Grace brought you to the place of closeness and intimacy with God. Why would you return to, or continue in the law?

"His grace is central to everything."

Grace Aligns All Creation

Creation is out of alignment and does not operate in the way the Father intended, when His throne is not at it's very center. It is essential for the throne of God to be the absolute center of the Messenger, Message, Motivation, Mission and Multitude to alleviate the Mess. This is the central theme of this book.

The letter to the Hebrews reveals a glimpse of Heaven and states;

> *"Let us therefore come boldly to the **throne of grace**, that we may obtain mercy and find grace to help in time of need." (Heb 4:16)*

The throne is a place of eternal grace and the epicenter of all creation. Therefore, His grace is central to everything. I cannot preach what is surely not grace and expect lives to be realigned correctly to God's Word and will. That is just not possible. For all things to be realigned and restored according to Gods plan and blueprint, then grace is not a suggestion of something that might be 'cool' or a good idea for me to apply to my life, but is instead a '**must**' for me to place at the very core of my belief system.

The writer exhorts us to come to the throne with boldness. The revelation of Grace makes me bold in God's presence, because everything is based upon His goodness and work, not mine. Because it is all based on Him, not me, then I can relax, because He is perfect and faithful. If I am under the law when I approach Him, then I will come to Him, not based upon His finished work in Christ, but based upon how well I have or haven't done. Since I am imperfect, then I stand upon shaky foundations and am not confident before Him. When based on the work of Jesus, then I can approach Him any and every day, knowing securely it is always a great day for me.

> "but **grow** in the grace and knowledge of our Lord and Savior Jesus Christ." (2 Pet 3:18)

I was born a boy and grew into a man. I had no choice in this process, my body just grew. I was born a child, but it was my choice to grow into a mature adult. I have met many a childish person in an adult body. They grew on the outside but not on the inside.

Peter urges us to grow up, come to a place of maturity in knowing, understanding and applying the grace of Jesus. It is such a sad realization, that so many have faithfully read their Bibles daily, have heard thousands of sermons, read hundreds of books and yet, they are still babies living under, and regurgitating, the letter of the law. They have not grown up in grace.

When I hear Christians telling others the do's and don't of being a good Christian, then I am instantly aware that the individual is still immature in Christ. The burdening of people with rules, regulations and rituals is not grace at work, but law. When we forbid people to listen to certain music, eat certain foods or wear certain items, then it reveals how the spirit of legalism is alive and well in us. People will go to Hell because they did not believe in or receive God's free gift of salvation through Christ, not because they ate some shellfish, drank coffee, alcohol, smoked a pipe or have a tattoo and other such things forbidden under the law. This sort of teaching returns the

Church back under the basic principles of the law based life, that
Jesus delivered us from (Col 2:8,20).

The message of the New Testament and New Covenant is clear. Grace
is the truth and is the gospel (Acts 20:24). Therefore, everything else
is the deception and another gospel (Gal 1:6), not the one that flows
out of Heaven. The Law was in place until the One it pointed to
arrived. He did, 2000 years ago. Now we preach Christ. We preach
Christ is the Lamb who takes away our sin. We preach Christ crucified,
dead, buried, resurrected and ascended, with victory over all sin, and
death now has no victory. Now we preach we are in Christ, therefore
in Christ we stand and are clothed in His righteousness and when the
Father looks at us He sees Christ! Now we preach if we are in Christ,
then we have overcome sin (1John 3:6)

John declared Jesus to be '*full of grace*' and grace is the manifestation
of His truth. If you wish to minister truth, then minister the
understanding of grace. How can we expect the power of God's grace
to flow in and through us, if the message we communicate is not
the complete truth? How can God back up and fulfill His Word, if
what we preach is actually the Law? When you dislocate a joint, you
immediately lose the strength and power of the limb, because it is out
of alignment to where it was meant to be. The moment you relocate
it, the power and strength returns. When there is so little evidence
of the power of God flowing in the Church, then I believe we can
recognize, something needs realigning. The power and ability of the
Spirit will flow, when the Word we preach on earth is in alignment
with the one spoken from the throne of God.

Follow Me!

*"Then He said to them, "Follow Me, and I will make you fishers
of men." (Matt 4:19)*

"Follow Me!" simply means we are to follow the person of Jesus
Christ, the Son of God. We are not called to follow a man, woman,

a religious system of rules, regulations and rituals, nor an earthly institution or organization. We are to follow Him. From the very beginning of His time on earth, Jesus called people into a personal relationship with Himself. This is the very foundation of the Church. He lived, died and was resurrected for one purpose;

> *"and **by** Him to reconcile all things **to Himself, by Him**, whether things on earth or things in heaven, having made peace through the blood of His cross. And you, who once were alienated and enemies in your mind by wicked works, yet now He has reconciled in the body of His flesh through death, to present you holy, and blameless, and above reproach in His sight.." (Col 1:20-22)*

Do you see this? His purpose and work is to bring everyone and everything back into relationship with Him, by Himself. He has paid every price necessary and is personally working today, to bring everyone and everything into reconciliation with Himself. This is God personally involved with you, doing the work Himself.

The mess, created by Lucifer's rebellion in Heaven and the yielding to temptation by Adam and Eve, disconnected everything from the Creator, and chaos flooded into creation. The reconciliation of all things to Christ, is the way He brings everything back into alignment and the door of chaos is finally closed and order in the house will be restored. The essence of God's message will always return man back to God. The lie always distances the relationship with God and man.

Whenever I am preaching, or listening to another preacher, I am constantly asking myself, 'is this message drawing people to Him, or distancing them from Him?' The gospel always draws people to the Father reminding them of His goodness and grace. Religion reminds people of their sin and the wrath of God, making them believe they are unacceptable in the Fathers presence.

Sin is not the problem. Jesus paid for it 2000 years ago. It was wiped out from before God at Calvary. The issue is do you believe the truth or the lie?

*"Then Jesus said to them again, "Most assuredly, I say to you, I am
the door of the sheep. **All** who ever came **before Me are thieves
and robbers**, but the sheep did not hear them. I am the door. If
anyone enters by Me, he will be saved, and will go in and out and
find pasture. The thief does not come except to steal, and to kill,
and to destroy. I have come that they may have life, and that they
may have it more abundantly." (John 10:7-10 NKJV)*

I want you to stop for a moment and contemplate this next statement,
in order to absorb the depths of it's truth. It has huge ramifications
on the way you believe, live and the message you communicate from
this moment onwards. Here it is:

Everything taught or established as the way to God, or the way to
please Him, before Jesus, was a thief and a robber! Nothing and no-
one else, but Him alone, is the doorway to the Father and never has
been.
The Law could never open the closed door between God and man. It
continually reminded the people that it was sin that closed the door
and only a sinless, perfect person had the key to unlock and open it.
Jesus is the key and the door. His offering of His perfect life, because
He is God the Son, turned the lock and the door opened.

A pick-pocket is a thief who steals from you when you don't even
realize it. Oh how this is so true of the subtle and deceiving way Lucifer
has hoodwinked so many people. He has infiltrated Christianity and
perverted it. He has deceived people into believing their salvation is
dependent upon something they do. These preachers move people
away from living by faith in the grace of God and into the same
erroneous teachings the Scribes and Pharisees taught, that Jesus
spoke against so vehemently. It has all been done with such slow and
subtle changes, shrouded with such religious garb, that it seems like
the truth, when it is actually the lie. Then, when someone stands up
and shouts out 'thief,' they are attacked ferociously and declared to be
a dangerous person to be avoided at all costs.
The pick-pocket was so good, that he stole the truth away from the

Church, replaced it with error, convincing them it was the gospel and when exposed makes the one telling the truth look like the deceiver! It is the art of the great illusionist.

"They rejected Him and continued the 'system'."

Religion - the Ancient Illusion!

When Jesus declared that everything that ever came before Him was nothing but a thief and a liar, He was talking to a nation of people who had all the history of the Tabernacles, the Temples, their furnishings, systems of sacrifices, feasts, the priests and their dress codes. For thousands of years the nation had operated within it's structure and Law. This 'new' preacher now declared that they were being deceived by believing that these things could give them right-standing with God. If the Scribes and Pharisees were not antagonized enough already, then they must have been nearly frothing at the mouth when He said;

"I am the way, the truth, and the life. No one comes to the Father except through Me" (John 14:6)

Not through the Law, the system of worship, sacrifices, rituals, special feast days, circumcision, robes, collars, incense or altars. Just Him. Everything else was a snare!
Jesus is the Truth. The legalistic leaders in Israel, reacted and planned His execution immediately. They were intrenched in the legalistic and systematic religion more than the truth and grace of the Messiah and Savior. The message was clear to all. Jesus was the long awaited Messiah and Savior. The Message and the Method He would use to

bring salvation and deliverance for them, did not fit their firmly held doctrinal views. It was to be based upon His work, not mans. It was based upon faith in His completed work, so all could be saved, by calling upon His Name, not by trusting in a genealogy proving they were of Jewish lineage. The message of Jesus, which has never changed, revealed that man could not claim salvation by natural birthright, or by being of the lineage of Abraham, or because they externally kept the Law. His words *"No man comes to the Father, but by Me,"* (Jn 14:6) cut to the heart of all that the system proclaimed. It made null and void their total religious concept, with it's accompanying activities, in the speed of light. He knew His words would bring the wrath of the whole religious spirit of a nation against Him. Yet, He was telling the truth.

You and I must not live in the place of compromise, wanting the Old and New to operate together. The New Testament gospel is the removal of the old and the establishing of the new;

> *"But now the righteousness of God **apart from the law** is revealed, being witnessed by the Law and the Prophets, even the righteousness of God, **through faith in Jesus Christ, to all** and on all **who believe**. For there is no difference; for all have sinned and fall short of the glory of God, being **justified freely by His grace** through the redemption **that is in Christ Jesus,"** (Ch 3:21-24)*

> *"having wiped out the hand-writing of requirements that was against us which was contrary to us, and has taken it out of the way, having nailed it to the cross." (Col 2:14)*

The perfect Law, written by His own finger, is no longer against you - it has gone.

> *"Having disarmed principalities and powers," (v 15)*

Grace disarms the demonic spirit world. If you turn away from believing the gospel of grace, you return to the law. Instantly, you will return to the bombardment of guilt and condemnation. Why? You threw away trusting in His righteousness, imputed to you by grace, and have returned to the foolishness of trying to become righteous through fulfilling the Law, which is impossible for man to fulfill and has been fulfilled by God for you. Lucifer is re-armed when we allow ourselves to be dis-robed of His righteousness.

I urge you, please read Galatians Chapter 3 and understand that Paul calls the Galatians 'foolish' because they were being turned away from grace and back to the Law. The Galation, Gentile Christians, were being taught by Jewish Christians, that it is God's will to mix faith in Christ with fulfilling the Law. What an abomination to God.

> *"Are you so foolish? Having begun in the Spirit, are you now being made perfect by the flesh?......... Therefore He who supplies the Spirit to you and works miracles among you, does He do it by the works of the law, or by the hearing of faith?—.......... Therefore know that only those who are of faith are sons of Abraham. But that no one is justified by the law in the sight of God is evident, for "the just shall live by faith." ....Christ has redeemed us from the curse of the law, having become a curse for us," (Gal 3:3,5,7,11,13)*

The Enemies of Grace

The New Testament shows three religious groups of people who get agitated and ultimately reject the message of grace. It seems to have always been this way. It makes me ask myself, if these three sections of people are not reacting and trying to come against the gospel we preach, then what gospel are we preaching?

> *"Then He went into the Temple and began driving out those who bought and sold in it, saying to them, "It is written, 'My house is a house of prayer, but you have made it a den of thieves.' " And He was teaching daily in the Temple. But the **chief priests**, the **scribes** and the **leaders** of the people sought to destroy Him, and*

were unable to do anything, for all the people were attentive to hear Him." (Mk 11:15-18)

This passage reveals there was a trading happening within the Temple system. It was the religious center and financial exchange of the day. Individuals traveling some distance, came in with money and purchased animals for sacrifice, saving them the hassle of bringing their own animal from long distances. Their money was exchanged for a sacrifice they would offer, to pay for sin or to declare their thankfulness to God, so the Law would be fulfilled. The exchange rate would depend upon availability, supply and demand, just as business operates so often today. It seems such a reasonable way to do things, so why did Jesus react so violently, using a whip to drive them all out of the Temple?

Did you notice a small but explosive word I used to describe their mode of operation? It was an *'exchange.'* The religious system always convinces people to exchange God's way for mans. Jesus is Grace and truth, who has always been greater than the Law. Grace and truth stood in the Temple, yet they continued their exchanging the offered relationship with God through Him, preferring to stay with a system of religion which could never achieve the goal. Though He was right there in front of them, in the Temple, still they rejected Him and continued the 'system.'

He blatantly and unapologetically, drove that attitude and spirit out of the place of worship. The Temple was built to reflect Him. Yet it didn't. He came to change the whole thing, to bring it into alignment with Himself, yet they rejected His realignment and kept the old order and system.

We see clearly, from His reaction, what God thinks about the exchanging of His grace for works that fulfill the Law. Even after He cleansed the Temple and then tore apart the veil, they rapidly sowed it back up and returned to the old system, totally rejecting what He was doing. This should wake all of us up to the power and workings of the old religious system. Like someone with an addictive spirit, people caught up in the spirit of religion can continually turn away from grace and truth and return to Law and works. When offered liberty, they prefer instead the trappings of bondage to an old wineskin and sadly lose all He is pouring out.

As Jesus left Jerusalem the disciples pointed out to Him how magnificent the Temple and all it's surrounding buildings looked. Probably with a deep sense of sadness, Jesus turned and said;

> *"Do you see all these things? Assuredly, I say to you, not one stone shall be left here upon another, that shall not be thrown down..............take heed that no-one deceives you." (Matt 24:2-4)*

He was prophesying the complete destruction of the physical legal religious system. Be not deceived my friend, the religious system will deceive people and 'hoodwink' them back into something Jesus died to set us free from.

The world wasn't forever changed because Jesus preached a great message. It was changed because He was the message of God personified. His life was the message. He didn't preach grace and truth, He **was** grace and truth in action. They literally experienced God's ultimate expression of Himself in the flesh. The Holy Spirit desires to do this in His Church, so that grace and truth will not be a theological disposition, or a great set of sermons, but the words used by those around us to describe what they discovered God to be like, because they have tasted and seen Him in us. The Message must do it's work and bring the Messenger into alignment with the Message, for it to have it's intended impact and fruitfulness in the world.

CHAPTER 8

The Motivation

The Heart Of A Father!

When the **MESSENGER** and **MESSAGE** match the **MISSION**, to restore the **MESS** in the chosen **MULTITUDE**, using God's eternal **METHOD**, **MODEL** and **MOTIVATION**, delivered at the **MOMENT** of His prompting, it brings supernatural **MULTIPLICATION** and the realignment of all things, into His likeness.

In my first book, 'Don't Kick The Donkey-Ride it!' I share my personal experience about a miraculous change that came in my relationship with my father. When still a young boy, my father had been abused by his step-father. Because of this experience, it marred his perception of what a true father was like, therefore, effecting his relationship with me, influencing my perception of fatherhood also. Without realizing, I carried this misconception into my walk with God the Father, as a new believer. In my book, I share how God lovingly brought total healing and deliverance, to both of us in a truly miraculous and wonderful way. For the final 14 years of my father's life, he and I were able to know and experience, the real love between a father and his son.

My father was so happy to finally find God's healing and forgiveness and be free of all that 'stuff' that had messed up his heart for so many years. Our hearts had been out of alignment with each other, because they were out of alignment with the Father's. The moment they were re-aligned to God's heart and understanding of a true Father, then a miracle flowed and our own natural 'houses' came into order and there was peace.

Luke 4:18-19 is one of the key 'foundational' passages of the New Testament for my life. It describes what has moved my heart to say what I say and do what I do, for over 30 years. I am inwardly driven to see it fulfilled in my lifetime. Here's what it declares;

> *"The Spirit of the LORD **is** upon Me, because He **has** anointed Me **to preach** the gospel to the poor; He **has** sent Me **to heal** the brokenhearted **to proclaim** liberty to the captives and recovery of sight to the blind, **to set** at liberty those who are oppressed; **To proclaim** the acceptable year of the LORD."*

Saved For a Purpose

Many people are held captive by their 'stinking thinking!' They need the 'renewing of the mind' (Eph 4:22 - 24) so they can 'see' and perceive what is actually the truth. This is what happened for both me and my father. God, the Father, called us out of the prison of an old mindset, into the liberty found in Him.

The Spirit of God is within every believer to simply pronounce Jesus has set everyone free, so they can get up and walk out into a new life of His liberty. He called you out of darkness and into the Kingdom of His Son, so that He could anoint you and send you back into the darkness, as the light, to lead people out of the darkness. You were saved for a purpose. There is a supernatural work He desires to do through you dear reader, that effects homes, streets and neighborhoods around you.

Throughout the Bible we see God raise up Patriarchs, men and women who changed nations and even the course of history. Each had met with God. Each spoke of Him using a different perspective. Abraham knew Him to be 'Jehovah Jireh,' the God who provides (Gen 22:8). To Moses He was 'Jehovah Nissi' the Lord is the Banner over me' (Ex 17:15). To David He was ' Jehovah Raar,' the Lord my Shepherd (Ps 23). You can see this pattern all the way through the Old Testament.

When Jesus comes, His whole life and message revolved around the revelation that God was 'Father.' If Jesus, the perfect reflection of who God is, reveals that God is 'Father,' then we can safely take it that this is the highest and greatest revelation for us to grasp. It describes who God is, not just what He does. He is our Father, the originator, creator who provides safety and provision to each of His children. The word 'Father' carries with it all the meanings of what a perfect and true father is like. Jesus said, "*I and My Father are One.*" (John 10:30) meaning 'one and the same.' So when we see the words and actions of Jesus, we see a complete representation of what our Father in Heaven is like. He is no different.

Jesus is the complete Chief Cornerstone of all creation. Everything He did was to bring creation back into alignment. When His Spirit was given to the Church, seen in Acts Chapter 2, He was given to the Church, to bring everything into alignment. With what and whom?

The Father. This is the revelatory truth that heals, delivers and realigns all people and societies and brings Heaven to earth.

So it is not a coincidence that the apostles of Jesus were also known by the Church as the 'fathers of the faith.'

When God raises up leaders and ministries for His Church today, what sort of people do you think they should be? Thats right, you got it! They are to be spiritual 'fathers.' The gifts, anointing's and talents of God are wonderful. We need every one of them to do what God has called us to do. But if we don't have the presence and input of spiritual fathers in the Church, the House of God, then we will have a glorified orphanage. We will have gatherings of siblings and you know the squabbling that exists between siblings. Maybe thats why we have such divisions in the Church. Lack of genuine 'fathers ' in the faith. Real Daddies create the culture of the Kingdom in the home of God.

Greater Vision Produces Greater Mission

Paul is Titus' spiritual father. He has been discipled by Paul and has accompanied him on his travels. On one of their journeys, they visited the island of Crete. Paul was so concerned about the spiritual situation of the island, that he left Titus there and assigned to him the task of setting things in order.

> *"For this **reason** I left you in Crete, that you should **set in order** the **things that are lacking**, and appoint **elders** in every **city** as I **commanded you**." (Titus 1:5)*

In this passage Paul never once mentions the Church. He mentions the whole nation and the city, but not the Church. Traditional teaching has always seen the ministry gifts of Eph 4:11 as purely for the Church. But have you noticed both Jesus, our great apostle (Heb 3:1) and Paul, also an apostle, went further than effecting the Church. Both radically effected the whole of their society. It says of Jesus;

*"God so loved the **world** that He gave His only begotten Son."
(John 3:16)*

God's purpose of sending Jesus was to effect the whole **world**, not just a synagogue in Nazereth. How did we miss this whole concept of ministry and Church life?
His mission was bigger. His sole purpose was to make sure His Message and Ministry would reach the whole world. It has. We have to awaken to a greater mission in life, than purely entertaining the troops inside the building every week. We are called to equip and send the troops, not entertain them.

Paul, an apostle, raised up spiritual 'sons.' In due season, he released those sons into the ministry, having already equipped them. He left Titus in Crete for a reason. He didn't abandon him, but left him there on purpose, with a purpose. The purpose? To set everything that was out of order, back into order. Whose order? The Father's! The things out of order in the nation, were actually preventing people receiving the abundance of God into their lives. They needed to be aligned, not to a theology, nor a Church organization, but a Father. He is the Life-giver, the source of Life, the originator. When they align themselves to Him, the life within Him automatically begins to flow and fill creation with His likeness.

Have you never noticed these verses?

*"a land in which you will eat bread without scarcity, in which you will **lack nothing**;" (Deut 8:9)*

*"and likewise of the fish, **as much as they wanted**." (John 6:11)*

*"not willing that **any** should perish," (2 Pet 3:9)*

This reveals the heart of God towards all people. He doesn't want one person to lack or perish. He wants **all** to *"prosper and be in health"*

(3 John 1:2). He desires to fill everything and everyone with His abundance and likeness.

Our life vision must be much much bigger. Only when our vision matches up to God's, will our hearts be filled with 'missions' to match the vision. Remember, I said in an earlier chapter, the vision is eternal and heavenly, whilst the mission is the earthly and temporal way we achieve the vision. God's vision is to bring all creation back into alignment with Himself. The mission He gives us, is the multitude of ways we reach creation to see it restored and realigned to His likeness. If the mission in our heart does not need the supernatural intervention of God to make it happen, then it is probably not of God, because it is not big enough. If it doesn't take us out of our comfort zones, outside the walls of the Church building and radically impact the society around us, then we probably need to come before God, for Him to open our eyes and imagination, to see and believe the way He does. If it doesn't consume you constantly, then it is just a dream, not a vision.

When it is truly birthed by the Spirit, then your mission in life will fill your heart with an all consuming passion, which is so contagious, that others will want to come and do it with you. It will not need a promised salary or a title to motivate you. You'll be so motivated that you would gladly work a job to pay for the mission out of your own pocket (Acts 18:3-4). When Saul met Jesus on the road to Damascus, it stopped him in his tracks. He could no longer live or believe as he did up to that moment. Meeting Jesus changed his world forever. He gave the rest of his days trying to fill his world with everything he experienced on that encounter. He met Jesus in all His glory. What he experienced conditioned how he lived and what he built everywhere he went. It was an encounter with the vision of Heaven and it released in him a mission to live for.
Jesus, and His apostles, impacted society on hilltops, highways and houses. They invaded every sector of society. The sick were healed, the dead raised, the hungry fed, the blind saw, the disabled made whole, the mentally insane brought back to their right minds. They

even impacted the natural elements of the world. Storms were stilled, water walked upon, walls walked through, people appearing and disappearing, fish and bread multiplied. They didn't just invade Church life. They invaded life. They didn't bring the world in, they took the Church out!

Have you ever wondered why these people groups were so often hostile towards them? Just think about this a moment. The sick paid for their treatment (Luke 8:43). Jesus, and the apostles, healed them all for free. They emptied cities of sickness and disease and by doing so, emptied the pockets of those charging for treatment. Do you really think the medical sector were thrilled with their impact?

"Jesus is the complete Chief Cornerstone of all creation."

The work of the local undertaker plummeted when they came to town. Jesus messed up the financial markets by cleansing the Temple of it's thievery and by Paul casting out a demon in a young fortune teller who guided the whole business community (Acts 16:16-24). The local food stores had to put up with Jesus feeding thousands with a few loaves and fishes. The fishing industry had to cope with supernatural catches of fish. How could they compete?

They emptied synagogues. When people left the synagogues their tithes and talents went with them. It would have caused tension then as it does now. The psychiatric and counseling rooms were not needed, because demons were cast out and people restored to their right minds. Every sector in the nations, was radically impacted through the power of the Spirit. This is the ministry of the apostles. If we receive and allow apostles into our ministries today, they will bring the Church back into alignment for this to happen once again.

Elders and Spiritual Fathers

Paul was aware that the things that were 'lacking' were just the result of things not properly 'set in order.' He knew if things were put into order, all that was lacking would begin to manifest. We don't know specifically what Paul was referring to, because he doesn't mention it in the letter to Titus. But it does show us a principle.

If Heaven's culture and the attributes of God's likeness are lost in a nation, then they will return when apostles are released to set things back in order. Paul continues to say;

"appoint elders in every city as I commanded you."

Staring back at us, from within these few words, is the crux of the reason why the island was lacking and why today, the Church is not having the impact in the world the way God always intended.

Firstly, Paul says 'as I commanded you.' A command is not a suggestion, or a hint. You do not 'command' anyone, unless there is a relationship that allows for it. Titus was Paul's spiritual son. Titus travelled with Paul purposely to learn from this wise master builder. He was Paul's disciple. His apprentice. Part of life's lesson for every 'son,' is to yield their independent spirit and submit it to fulfill a command given them through their 'father.' This is the only way to learn submission to true godly authority. You must first come under authority, before you can exercise it over anyone or anything else. Lack of submission to godly order in the home and the Church is why nations are lacking the glory of God's likeness. It will not come to the world before it comes back to the home of every believer.

Secondly, Paul instructs Titus to establish 'elders' in every city. This is not referring to elders who are appointed in the local Church to oversee meetings. This ministry is to have a city-wide influence. This is not about having the title 'elder,' but about the spiritual authority and ability, an elder is meant to operate in.

Both John and Peter were apostles. Yet they call themselves a 'fellow-elder' or 'elder' (1 Pet 5:1; 2 John 1:1). This reveals to us, that the early

Church operated with the understanding that the five-fold ministries, shown in Eph 4:11, was also known as part of the eldership over a city or region. These ministries are gifted, anointed and sent of God with His grace to equip the people for the work of ministry, to edify (build up) the whole Body of Christ, to bring the unity of the faith, raise the Church up to the stature of the fullness of Christ.

They worked together and built together. They didn't segregate the Church, they kept the unity. They didn't build their own streams or denominations, separated from others. They were and still are, the Generals of God's army. These are the fathers in His House, bringing order and putting everything into alignment wherever they go. These are the ones sent of God to raise up the spirit of 'sonship' in the Church. Slaves only do what they are told. Servants do what they are paid or rewarded for. But a son will do it because it pleases the father and he has caught the fathers spirit. My passion is for you to catch the spirit of your heavenly Father and help you see you are a 'son.' Sons learn from fathers and fathers raise sons, giving them the ability to go out and become fathers themselves.

Raise, Reproduce, Release

I love my kids so much. But did not raise them to live under my roof, in my pocket, doing only what I do. I want them to have their own home, family and impact on this world. I have failed as a father if my focus is to keep them at home with me. My job is to raise them, reproduce maturity in them equipping them for life and release them to have their own family elsewhere. The Church needs to follow this pattern.

It is not how many come in and stay that shows our fruitfulness to God, but how many go back out to repeat the process for themselves. Churches that have tens of thousands of believers going through the doors each week to watch a few dozen do the 'ministry' is not being fruitful. It is spiritual constipation. Everything is going in and nothing coming back out. I always tell congregations that God is very wise. When He made mankind He gave us a hole at the top for food to go in, and a hole at the bottom for the it to come back out!!! If it all goes in but nothing ever comes out, then we will get toxic poisoning and die. Sadly, too many Christians and Churches suffer with spiritual constipation. I am praying that this book acts like a spiritual enema to many people, loosing them from stagnation and wanting more and more revelation and more personal prophesies, whilst all around them darkness controls their region, multitudes slipping into Hell without Christ.

Elders are spiritual fathers in God's House. New Testament eldership is not a title or position. It is a function and an office. It has purpose. The grace of God is released through them to protect and provide, not subdue and control.
When the model of leadership in Church is out of alignment with the New Testament pattern, then the Church will be out of alignment, because the Church reflects it's leadership, just as a family reflects the parents. When the Church is out of alignment to God's heavenly pattern, then the world will be also, because Jesus is the cornerstone to the Church and through her, to creation.

Fathers Are Overseers

I wish to close this chapter with just a word of wisdom to you, regarding the issue of authority and submission in the Church.
New Testament elders are 'overseers' (Acts 20:28; 1 Pet 5:2). This Greek word means, 'careful over-sight, to look upon, see-over, care for.' This word makes no reference to a sense of lordship over the flock of God. We are instructed **not** to control from a position of lordship.
In the days of Jesus, a shepherd would construct a circular sheep-pen from stones. It would have no gate and no roof. The shepherd, or under shepherd would sleep in the gateway at night to prevent wolves or bears from getting to the sheep. This reveals the level of care the leaders should express towards the flock. A willingness to fight off anything that may harm the sheep.

By having no roof over the sheep, means the sheep could look up to the heavens freely, with no barriers, at any time. A shepherd and leader has no authority to get between THE Shepherd and His sheep. The role of leadership is always to bring all the sheep into a deep personal relationship with their True Shepherd, with an ability to look to God, hear and obey Him for themselves.

The Old Testament High Priest was the intercessor, standing between God and His people. You could not approach God personally. The High Priest did it for you. Christ is our eternal High Priest, who interceded and paid the price to reconcile you. Now you are in direct relationship with the Father and don't even need to ask Jesus to ask the Father on your behalf (John 16:23). You need no priest, pastor or prophet to approach Him or hear from Him. You have His Spirit within you. You can know Him and hear Him for yourself.

No-one needs a leader's 'permission' to do what God told them to do. They may need the help, wisdom and support of leadership, but not permission. Every believer is to grow up in Christ, take responsibility to hear God for ourselves and be obedient to His will and Word.

Someone's faithfulness in obeying the leading of the Spirit is not an act of rebellion, even if it differs to what a leader believes is right. They are not in rebellion, but in submission to God's Word, which is a higher authority.

> *"My sheep hear My voice, and I know them, and they follow Me." (John 10:27)*

CHAPTER 9

The Method

Tru Discipleship of All Believers

When the **MESSENGER** and **MESSAGE** match the **MISSION**, to restore the **MESS** in the chosen **MULTITUDE**, using God's eternal **METHOD**, **MODEL** and **MOTIVATION**, delivered at the **MOMENT** of His prompting, it brings supernatural **MULTIPLICATION** and the realignment of all things, into His likeness.

"to set at liberty those who are oppressed, to proclaim the acceptable year of the Lord." (Luke 4:18-19; expansions from Strong's Concordance)

The Spirit of Liberty

In this quote of Luke 4:17-18 the writer uses, in it's original language, the sense that the captive is already freed, the chains broken and the cell door open. Now someone just needs to tell them they are free. Some remain 'prisoners' all their lives to sin, guilt, sickness, debt and such things, all because of their own 'stinking thinking.'
When you first share with them that Jesus has liberated their entire life, as well as their spirit, from the curse of sin, sickness, shame and everything else that has bound them, they initially believe you to be seriously in error. They have believed the lie for so long, they now believe the truth to be the lie.

Luke's gospel declares the reason why the Spirit is upon Jesus. He is acting as the vessel for the Spirit to flow through Him. It is definitely the work of the Spirit, not Jesus. His own declaration confirms this;

*"Then Jesus answered and said to them, "Most assuredly, I say to you, **the Son can do nothing of Himself,** but what He sees the Father do; for whatever He does, the Son also does in like manner." (John 5:19)*

"but the Father who dwells in Me does the works." (John 14:10)

So this work of liberating people, is both the Mission and Method of God. If this is the Mission and Method of the Spirit, then it must become ours. What is the Method Jesus reveals? It is to do what God is doing and say what God is saying! Simple? Work where God is working. Do it the way God is wanting it done. This instantly means an intimate, sensitive and trusting co-operation with God, is necessary. Being 'in tune' with the Spirit brings life and light to where death and darkness have reigned. It also tends to put you on a collision course with traditional man made strategies and systems that have dictated the Church institution for so many years.

It is really good to hear what God 'said' in the past. But it is essential for us to hear what He 'says' right now (Rev 2:7). One speaks of learning from the past, the other reveals obedience to God's present day leading. If we don't learn to hear and promptly obey His leading, then the anointing will not flow and bring Heaven to earth, right into that moment.

The Greek wording *'set at liberty'* carries the meaning of 'release from obligation.' Obligation to what? To all that oppresses the person! WOW! Jesus is declaring that people feel obligated to remain under things that oppress them, when they don't need to. This means it is also our ministry and mission.

> *"Come to Me, all you who labor and are heavy laden, and I will give you rest........"For My yoke is easy and My burden is light."* *(Matt 11:28,30)*

Easy Ministry

People in leadership and ministry often tell me they are 'burnt out.' When ministry becomes an obligation, 'heavy' and burdensome, then stop it immediately, because you are operating in the flesh, not the anointing. Jesus said His work is easy, light. Easy ministry happens when we stop trying to do it and let Him do it. He said "I will build My Church" (Matt 16:18). He didn't say you would do it. So how does He do it if He is in Heaven? He does it through the ministries, gifts and anointing of the Spirit, given to every individual.

When the person gifted of God for the task, is in the right place to do it, then the grace of God flows and the work is done. The Greek word for the 'gifts' of the Spirit is 'charisma', which comes from the root Greek word 'Charis,' meaning 'grace.' Operating in the gifts and ministry function God has given you, allows His grace and ability to flow through you to accomplish the task. So it really isn't you doing the work at all.

The ministry of the Spirit is the evidence of His dwelling in you and it flows through you whenever you are simply being who He made you to be, wherever you are. He travels wherever you go and will flow anywhere at anytime, no matter how you feel, or what day or time it is. It is so silly for us to think the anointing and calling upon us is to just operate within the four walls of a building called 'Church,' at a set time each week. What a tragic waste of His presence and ability in our lives.

Let me ask you a question. Is it better to work where the anointing in your life flows or doesn't flow? It is obviously better where it flows. Then, is it better to remain working within the traditional concept of Church for years, where the anointing within you doesn't flow, or somewhere else where it does? If you hesitated for one moment in thinking about your answer, then there's your problem. You feel obligated to the system of Church, not free to respond to the leading of His Spirit. You are not alone. This burden of 'obligation' has entrapped the church for centuries. When we are 'obligated' to do what isn't fruitful, then we must see that we are not doing what God wants us to do. There is more ministry opportunity outside the four walls of a building, than ever there will be in a Church meeting.

"Work where God is working."

Many believers in Christ are enslaved and obligated to many things preventing them walking in the fulness of all God has provided for them. His desire? To set them free.

Relationship Or Religion?

*"If you abide in **My** word, you are **My disciples** indeed, And you shall know the truth and the truth shall make you free..........*
*Therefore, if **the Son** makes you free, you shall be free indeed."*
(John 8:31-32)

Notice the response of the crowd to His declaring this statement. They answered Him saying;

*"We are Abraham's descendants, and have **never been in bondage** to anyone." (v 33)*

They were so rooted in religious deception, that when the Truth stood in front of them they didn't recognize Him or receive Him. The Jewish people had received the Word of God from Abraham to John the Baptist. Their problem was not in the measure of the Word preached to them, but in the fact they never lived by personal faith in the Word they heard! (Heb 4:1-2)

One stood amongst them, who instead of just listening to what God had said and done in the past, decided to live His life hearing and doing what He heard and saw the Father saying and doing today. He did it outside of their system and they ridiculed, slandered and crucified Him. They rejected His way, preferring to keep to their old wineskin. The ordinary people of Israel flocked to follow Jesus, in such a manner, that it was the religious leaders who became His hostile accusers, eventually arranging His death. They were afraid of Jesus' Method, because their old wineskin was being replaced by personal, intimate relationship with God the Father, through Jesus Christ and taking people away from the control and structure of the 'system.' The Pharisees created, intimidated and threatened Jesus, the apostles and all who followed them. Why? Because they were afraid of the collapse of the old order and with it, their influence and control. They lashed out at Jesus and the apostles, believing them to be the culprits of this act of rebellion. When in fact is was the God they said they served, was bringing the changes.

Jesus didn't come to establish a new religion. Nor fix a broken one. He came to destroy altogether, the concept of any religion being the way to God.

A New Pattern Emerges

*"And he departed from there and entered the house of a certain man named Justus, one who worshipped God, whose **house was next door to the synagogue**. Then Crispus, the ruler of the synagogue, believed on the Lord with all his household. And many of the Corinthians, hearing and believing were baptized......... And he continued there for a year and six months, teaching the word of God among them." (Acts 18:7-11)*

*"And he (Paul) went into the synagogue and spoke boldly for three months, reasoning and persuading concerning the things of the kingdom of God. But when some were **hardened and did not believe**, but spoke evil about 'The Way' before the multitude , he departed from them and **withdrew the disciples**, reasoning in the school of Tyrannus. And this continued for two years, so that all who dwelt in Asia heard the word of the Lord Jesus Christ, both Jews and Gentiles." (Acts 19:8-10)*

Paul's leaving an old 'wineskin' and establishing a new one, seemed to cause him no problem whatsoever. Unlike many today too afraid to make necessary changes. Paul knew the dangers of the old wineskin from painful experience. I am sure he thanked God every day of his life, that He had radically freed him from the dying system and baptized him into the wonderful liberty of God's Grace that he now experienced.

The amazing consequence of leaving the old wineskin, was the covering of the whole of Asia Minor with the gospel in just 3 years. Why would we stay trapped in an old wineskin, when such incredible impact is available. One man could never have achieved this result. So, how did it happen?

Paul changed the method. The current system needed to be changed. But try as he might, the old system did not desire to change. So, he simply stopped trying to change it and started a new method.

Paul didn't take people into a religious system that was dead, he brought them out of it. He went into the synagogue, teaching the truth found in Christ, in the power of the Spirit. When it was rejected, he withdrew from the synagogue all those that had received his message and began a discipleship group, even in the house next door!
He shows no fear of what people within the old wineskin may say about him. He lived to please God. His love of God was greater than any fear of man. He didn't have time to waste in playing Church politics. His eyes were upon the Mission of God and if the Method used was a hindrance to the goal, he was willing to discard it and use a new one that accomplished the task. Such boldness.

Paul's attitude was one of, 'if the method worked for Jesus, then it will work for me.'
He discipled his followers with the fundamental understanding that they are called to be obedient to Christ. He equipped them to preach the gospel of the Kingdom of God, with signs following and to replicate themselves wherever they went. The goal was the discipleship of all people, not the establishing of a system or organization that revolved around any man or woman. It revolved around everyone's knowing and hearing the Word of God and obeying the leading of the Holy Spirit and to reproduce this same principle in others.
For us to reach our world with such astonishing speed and impact that the early church did, then we **must** return to the same method revealed by Jesus.

What Works In The Home, Will Work In The Church

The early Church grew and spread across the known world due to the persecution they experienced. As they fled, so they influenced the communities by establishing discipleship groups wherever they were. This was good, but was not intentional growth or influence. It was a by-product of the persecution.

But Luke's writing of the Book of Acts shows Paul's method was not simply responding to accidental serendipity. Rather, his was the direct implementation of a spirit-led strategy. He did it on purpose. The Church today must be just as pro-active as Paul was in his day.

We must disciple new believers in a clearly defined systematic way, that enables them to lead someone to Jesus Christ and personally disciple the new believer, not bring them into a New Believers Class within the building called the Church. It is THE Church that is meant to be doing the discipling, not the institution.

The expected, normal way in life, is that when a couple have a child, they are responsible to raise it. Except in rare cases, we do not take a child from a family unit and raise it in an institution. God set this pattern and it is the way of life (PS 68:6; Acts 2:47). If it works in the home, then it will work in the Church. So why don't we follow this biblical model? The Church is a spiritual family. The foundational principles of Church life and home life are the same (1 Tim 3:4-5). This 'new' wineskin may break the mould of the old one we fight so much to continue, but what is our choice? The wineskin so predominantly evident today is failing. It will never achieve the goal of Christ which is to reach the whole earth with His Message. But if we are brave enough to make the necessary changes, become a 'mission' orientated people, where all are equipped and released to do the work of discipleship, then this world could be reached within one generation. My motto is "**100% of the Church does 100% of the ministry**."

What I am saying may not be 'politically correct' to the institution called 'the Church,' but I believe it needs to be said. Billions of people are going to hell, while the Church, who has been granted the grace to share the greatest message ever known in history, is ensnared by the fear of man, preferring instead to tow the party line!

It may be outrageous. It may challenge the standard method of most churches. But thats my point. I am not trying to save the institutional method, nor win a popularity contest. I am simply trying to get every believer back to living the normal Christian model, as shown in the New Testament. They are to be a disciple!

Turn The Light On

What would your town, or city look and feel like, if in the place of darkness, the Kingdom of Light was established? It would be Heaven on earth! Darkness is just the absence of light. When you turn on a light, you do not wait ten minutes while light and darkness battle for supremacy. There is no power contest. The moment the light is turned on, the darkness has gone. When the Church is hiding it's light under a bushel, inside their buildings, then nothing prevents darkness filling our streets and neighborhoods. It is time for every child of God to come outside the walls of the system and turn their light on!

This is the goal and mission of the Church. All projects and missions must have the achievement of this goal as its central purpose. To re-establish the order of God in every sphere of life. The bringing of people into our buildings as the ultimate focus and purpose of the Church must cease. Instead, the whole Church needs to return to the community to make the difference. We must flood society again with the evidence of His Kingdom. Instead of holding a healing meeting in the 'Church,' why don't we equip the whole Church to go out into the community they live and work in, to pray for the sick wherever they find the sick living?

Look how two baby followers of Jesus, were used of God to effect their whole community;

> *"The woman then left her waterpot, went her way **into the city**, and said to the men, "Come, see a Man who told me all things that I ever did. Could this be the Christ?" Then they went out of the city and **came to Him**..........Then they said to the woman,*

*"**Now we believe**, not because of what you said, for we ourselves have heard Him and we know that this is indeed the Christ, the Savior of the world." (John 4: 28-30, 42)*

*"Now the man from whom the demons had departed begged Him that he might be with Him. But Jesus sent him away, saying, "**Return to your own house, and tell** what great things God has done for you." And he **went his way and proclaimed throughout the whole city** what great things Jesus had done for him. So it was, when Jesus returned, that the multitude welcomed Him, for **they were all waiting for Him**." (Luke 8:38-40)*

This is the Method of Jesus. A woman of five marriages and now living with a partner, is confronted by Jesus with compassion and no judgment of her sin. In just a few minutes, was touched forever by the Savior's grace and returned to her community telling everyone she had found the Messiah. Everyone came to meet Him and believed on Him.

"Jesus didn't come to establish a new religion."

The Gaderene man had received a miracle and wanted to be part of Jesus' traveling 'ministry' team, Jesus declined his request for good reason. When Jesus returned to this area, some time later, a multitude were waiting for Him. Why? Because the young man remained in the area sharing what Jesus had done in his life. The crowd would not have been waiting for Jesus, if this man had not remained in his home town and region.

Neither of these two followers of Jesus, went through the six week 'New Believers Class' in the local church. They just naturally and simply shared Jesus wherever they went. Of course I believe in teaching and grounding new believers in the Word of God. But we mustn't think someone cannot be used of God until their theology or understanding is perfect.

There are some called of God to minister to the Church. But the majority of us are called to reach and minister to the world around us. We do not need 90% of the Church ministering to the Church and 10% ministering to the world. We need it the other way around.

Connect - Not Disconnect!

When a new believer comes to Christ, they possibly have between 30-50 good relationships with unsaved family and friends. But this is also the point when most Churches make a basic mistake. They get the person saved and immediately begin a program of integration for this new believer. New believers are instructed to attend the classes for new believers, water baptism, where they learn the basics of being a Christian and faithful member of the local Church. They are encouraged to attend all mid-week and Sunday services, which ensures to everyone else that they are 'committed' Christians (though the New Testament never asks for this). They may be placed into a small group system within the Church to be taught that they were saved with a purpose and that purpose is to serve the Lord, in the Church. Then they are encouraged to find a place to serve within the Church. Sound about right?

During this process they learn the Church dress code, that smoking, drinking alcohol and listening to 'worldly music' is forbidden because of it's dangers. In the end these once vibrant people have the 'cloned' look of the local Church they belong too. Slowly, but surely, we pull them out of the big bad dark world, where apparently, it is unsafe for anyone to remain in and we lovingly build a barrier around them to 'protect' them. It is called the local 'Church.'

After the new believer has done everything the Church has required, is a great attendee and asset in the Church, they find themselves disconnected from the family and friends network they once had. Then, they get preached at, that it is their responsibility to bring more unsaved people into the meetings!!! Well how can they? All the relationships they once had, have been dissolved by the 'system' of the Church. Now they look and talk like someone from a different world to the one they once lived in. They are an alien in their own community.

"Follow Me, and I will make you fishers of men." (Matt 4:19)

Fish do not leap out of the water, make their way across the fields to the home of a fisherman, to be caught. The fisherman goes to the fish. Fish eat when hungry. They only bite what they like to eat. Some fish are bottom feeders and some feed on the surface. Some fish are so clever, that fishermen have to dress to blend in with the bushes not to be seen. So, it is the fish that determines where the fisherman goes to fish, when they go, what bait is used and the way they fish. They even determine what they dress like!!

If you want to catch 'fish' for Jesus, you need to follow this same principle. The unsaved community in your area determines how, where and when you share the gospel with them and if you want to not 'spook' or frighten them off, then dress and act in a way that you blend in with their surroundings.

A pipe organ, a shirt and tie, or a twin set with high heels, are no more holy and acceptable to God than denim jeans, a t'shirt and a rock and roll band singing His praises. In fact the Father doesn't care what style of clothes you wear, or songs you sing. He does care about your obedience to His call to reach this world with His message.

It is time for us to actively remove every traditional barrier set up between us and the people we are trying to reach. Trying to get the unsaved into a building that doesn't look like anything they would normally go in, to sing songs with words that mean nothing to them, sung in styles they cannot relate to, to watch people behave in a way that seems foreign to them, is nearly always a fruitless activity. But asking them to come into your home for a meal isn't. That is really normal to them. It is non-threatening, because it is based on friendship, which leads to relationship and trust. Only when someone trusts you will they pour their lives out to you, drop down the drawbridge of their heart and invite you in. It takes time and friendship before they reach this place.

> *"go out quickly, into the streets and lanes of the city, and bring in here ... the poor* (spiritually), *and the maimed* (hurt by life) *and the lame* (those struggling to walk properly with God) *and the blind* (the lost). " *(Lk 14:21-24)*

When Jesus made this statement, He was sitting in a house, not a religious building. He was telling everyone (not just the evangelist who comes to town once a year), to reach out to these types of people and bring them into our homes and love them back to wholeness. Its time for us to use our homes as the place of worship, evangelism and the discipling of all who give their lives to Christ. It is time to walk our street(s) and sing God's Word over every home, shop, business premises and school, build friendship with and minister to them all. It is time to turn my personal light on in my neighborhood, not expect everyone else to do it for me.

At the end of this book you will find the *in*HOPE vision that will explain in more detail, how we believe the Lord will move to impact a nation. Please take time to read it. It may confirm what He has placed in your heart.

CHAPTER 10

The Model

The City-Wide Church

When the **MESSENGER** and **MESSAGE** match the **MISSION**, to restore the **MESS** in the chosen **MULTITUDE**, using God's eternal **METHOD**, **MODEL** and **MOTIVATION**, delivered at the **MOMENT** of His prompting, it brings supernatural **MULTIPLICATION** and the realignment of all things, into His likeness.

Everything Changes!

In my book 'Don't Kick The Donkey-Ride it!' and in the earlier chapter on 'The Moment,' I try to convey that the crucifixion of Jesus 2000 years ago, followed by an empty tomb, a constantly changing appearance of Jesus and an ascension was the ultimate game-changer. Everything changed. What the Father did through His Son made a demand upon everything to come into alignment with these changes.

A brief look at Israel's history will reveal to all, the sadness and calamity that follows, when His people do not move with His changes. It seems we don't like to change! We seem afraid to, maybe because we can't control the moment. But that's the point of all I write. The truth is, we have never been in control of anything. We just like to think we are. Change will happen in your life whether you like it or not, or want it or not. Life demands you to respond accordingly.

The New Testament was written for us to see clearly the wineskin changed forever. The physical and temporal buildings, sacrifices and clothing's of the Old Testament, are now changed to spiritual and eternal ones. It is now the priesthood of **all** believers who have been clothed with His garment of righteousness, not a few 'special' ones, robed in clerical attire.

The letter to The Hebrews is written to Jewish people converted to Christ, who have been infiltrated by teachers who are mixing the rituals of Judaism with the simple faith in Christ of Christianity. It systematically shows that in Christ we have a better everything. A better Passover Lamb and High Priest in Jesus. A better New Covenant which supersedes and replaces the Old Covenant, with better promises. We serve in the Heavenly Sanctuary, better than the earthly one. With better sacrifices of praise and worship flowing over the altars of our lips. The letter questions why the readers would turn their backs on all of this, to return to the rituals and systems of the Law and all it's trappings? The author appeals to them to remain faithful to simple faith in Christ. He is showing them the wineskin has changed. So embrace it.

When 90% of the Church's focus, resources and energy, revolve around keeping the system going and just 10% is used to reach those yet to hear the gospel, then you can see why the Church has become an organization instead of remaining heavens organism in the earth. I wonder what the picture would look like, if we turned those percentages around the other way? Oh yes, it would look just like Jesus and the New Testament Church wouldn't it!

"What man of you, having a hundred sheep, if he loses one of them, does not leave the ninety-nine in the wilderness, and go after the one which is lost until he finds it?" (Luke 15:4)

This is the model of Jesus. When the early Church followed His model, they saw hundreds of millions of people, come to a living faith in Christ, within 300 years. They were the greatest force in the earth. Every government and religious institution was afraid of them. Their influence was a counter-revolution to the establishment order. But it all came to a sudden grinding halt. Not through persecution, but through comfort. Not because they had lost their vision, but because their vision had been corrupted.
King Constantine demanded the Church be given the same rights as the world institutions and built huge buildings for them to meet in. He dressed Church leaders in special, high quality robes, to give them the same status as the university lecturers.
The Church fell into the trap. They turned inward, became institutionalized, more focused upon reaching the high mountain tops of power and acceptability in the eyes of the world, than reaching nations with the gospel.

Every revival or reformation since, has been a burst of Heaven's perspective and life, invading the Church to deliver it of the trappings of religious institutionalism that diminishes His power working through them. Some receive it and respond. Others reject it, preferring instead, the systems of religion. Tensions rise within the Church forcing people to eventually leave, gathering with others of like mind to begin new works. Why? Because the Wineskin changed and some would not change with it!

A Brand New Way

If all the governments of this world collaborated together, removed every Church building from the global Church and made it illegal for them to hold meetings in halls or use any religious titles, what would happen to the Church? How would it operate? What would happen with the tithes? How would we know who the leaders and ministries are? How would we fulfill the scripture '*do not neglect the gathering of the saints?*' Where and when would the Church gather? Who would make the appeals for salvation? Who would disciple these new converts? Ha Ha I can hear your brains whirling around as you ponder on the questions.

Well, how did the early New Testament believers do it all? They had these same questions. They were kicked out of the synagogues and Temple system. They had no liturgical, qualified and ordained leaders or priests. They had no titles or structure of rules and regulations. They had no buildings to maintain and operate, so what did they spend the tithes on?

We can clearly see from the Book of Acts and the letters of the apostles, that they seemed happy to be free of the 'system.' In fact they drew everyone out of it that they could. They were the fastest growing entity in the earth. The people honored them. They saw a constant outpouring of God's miracle power in signs and wonders everywhere they went. The Church flourished, crossing every known barrier and border. They adapted the presentation of the message to every situation, without ever compromising the gospel. People lived and died to propagate the gospel, counting it an honor to die for it. Each one of us that own a Bible, has it because blood was shed to get it to us.

This new Church didn't have a fancy name on a building. It had been nick-named 'The Way,' because this was the message they preached and the method they adopted. They met anywhere, at anytime necessary in order to spread the message, but especially operating in and through their homes. Their 'hub' was their home, not a Church building. Leaders had no titles. They understood the pastor, evangelist, apostle, teacher and prophet to be ministries and functions, not positions and titles. They had no division between Priests and Laity. No hierarchy. All were royal priests. They had no denominations or 'streams' of Churches.

"The Church flourished, crossing every known barrier and border."

Some have stated that I am against the local church. I am not against anything, I am 'for' something. I am 'for' having the expression of life Jesus died for us to have. I am for **being** the Church, not 'going' to Church. I am for the extension of His Kingdom to all people everywhere at all times. I am for having an expression of Church that allows for the lost and bewildered in life to experience the presence of God and the culture of His Kingdom. I am for the total unity of the House of God in a city, adorned with His gifts and fruits, rather than having glorious buildings adorned with lavish decorations, dotted all over the region, which the unsaved never enter. I am for having one building used to capacity by the whole Church, than a multitude of them dotted across a region, half empty. I am for helping every congregation in the city, to be fruitful in it's God given purpose and mission. I am 'for' the local Church, just not in the format and spirit it so often operates in today.

One Church, Many Locations

The New Testament Church had one leadership over the region. They had one church in many locations, all working together for the common good of the Kingdom of God. I am absolutely 'for' this kind of local Church. It is possible to obtain, if people are open to hear what the Spirit is saying today!

I passionately believe His earthly Church and Body must be drawn into alignment with His heavenly one, for Jesus only has one Church and one Body. It is eternal, glorious, victorious, contagious, relentless, unified and each earthly expression of it, is part of the whole one. Just the same as your body is made up of a multitude of parts, yet each one has the same life running through it and all cooperating for the whole body to work correctly. Jesus did not birth a divided Kingdom, Church or Body. We did this to Him all on our own. There's a way we can reverse this curse.

Real Communion

In 1Cor 11:17-34 we have Paul's teaching on the Lord's supper, or often known today as 'communion. It is now, so often, portrayed in a way that no longer resembles what Jesus instigated in the upper room, the night He was arrested. We are divided over it, rather than declaring our unity through it. Instead of it being an event that declares to the heavens and earth, our covenant love of Jesus and for each other, we have reduced it to an institutionalized ceremony, so 'holy' that normal people can't administer it. It is celebrated on special Sundays, held within our own Church buildings, taken separately, from others in the Body of Christ, who are not allowed to partake of it, because they are not of our doctrinal stand.

Now let us review Paul's teaching and see if what we do matches up with his instruction. Paul instructs us to 'come together.' This word means 'assemble, cohabitation, come with one another' and it speaks of 'being and building' together. It doesn't say at all in this passage that we take it with only those who believe what 'I' believe. How arrogant is that. I love my wife and family. I don't love them when they believe what I believe and not love them when they don't. I am called to love my enemies. If I cannot express this love to the Church, my spiritual brothers and sisters, how will I ever have the ability to love my enemies?

Paul speaks of not being surprised at hearing of them having divisions when they come together (v18). Then continues to show the divisions reveal who is 'approved' amongst them. The word 'divisions' is actually 'heresies,' implying those who divide or keep divided at this table of communion, are the heretics and not the 'approved' and genuine ones.

In v20 we are instructed to eat the Lord's supper, in one place. Once again it speaks of unity. Seeing they had no buildings where did this occur? The answer is anywhere. It makes no mention of what day or time because it doesn't matter. It is done 'whenever' or 'wherever' the Church meets together in unity. Most times it was part of a meal in a home, where the believers gathered for the teaching of the Word. At other times, the city-wide Church gathered in the open somewhere, to hear the reading of a letter that had arrived from one of the apostles.

Go Fetch Them To The Table

Paul rebukes people for eating before everyone has arrived, leaving some hungry (v21). I remember when growing up, that my mother would stand on the doorstep and call me, my brother and sister, to come for supper. My sister and I would run home, wash our hands and sit at the table ready to eat. The food was placed on the table in front of us. Then my mother would ask 'where's your brother?' We would respond 'No idea, out playing somewhere.' To my annoyance, my mother would command me to run and fetch him. I didn't want to, I was hungry and therefore complained to her. She would look at me and remind me, 'no-one begins until everyone is at the table together.' I was responsible to go and fetch whoever was missing from that table and do everything I needed to do to bring them to it. We could not partake of what was on the table until we all sat down to eat together.

I guess my mother got this understanding from Paul's instruction. Isn't this precisely what it is speaking of. It is not referring to a fragment of bread or cracker and a thimble full of juice. It is a table full of food. The Lord's Table is just the same. Is is absolutely laden with the very best of the very best He provides. His table is laden with miracles.

We are not to 'swag around' independently eating of His miraculous provision, not caring that the rest of the Church is left in need. One congregation may have an abundance of musicians, or teachers, whilst another part of the Body is limited in these areas. We cannot just sit back boasting in what we have, enjoying my abundance. We have the abundance, not because of anything we did to earn it. It was given by grace. It was given for us to share for the betterment of the whole church in the area, so that all parts of the body are healthy, not just one part.

We are responsible to bring all the Church together, to the same table and place of abundance, to enjoy it all together, so that no part of the Body lacks any good thing.

All the gifts, the ministries, the revelation and the talents are given to the Church for the common good (betterment) of the whole Church(v17) in your region. Jesus is the only one who had all the gifts, ministries and revelation. Yet, I cannot recall one place He uses any of them for His own betterment. He used all He had to bless others, that they may enjoy what He had. He brought the sick, diseased, broken, ostracized and guilty to His table (heart) and fed them all. When they left, they were all healed, delivered, whole and forgiven. This is the spirit of true communion.

When pastoring in Wales, the Church used to hold love feasts. It was our understanding of real communion. Everyone brought food and drink and placed it on the common table. The more affluent may have brought a slab of beef, whilst others unable to contribute much, brought a loaf of bread. Everyone contributed according to their ability and desire, some more sacrificial than others. Each brought enough for their family and one more person. **All** contributed something. Everyone would go around the table taking what food they wanted or needed. It was an open, common table. All were welcome, all contributed and all took what they needed. The whole Body contributed to the welfare of the whole Body, by each contributing what they had.

"He used all He had to bless others."

One summer's day my wider family all decided we should do a family picnic. On arrival at our arranged meeting place, each family unit put on the floor a blanket or rug, spreading out the food for lunch. My wife and I, sat on our blanket, along with our son Matthew who was just a couple of years old and began to eat. Suddenly, Matt got up and walked over to my sister's picnic. He looked over their food and helped himself to something he wanted. We all laughed. Then he did it again, this time on someone else's blanket. He did this all lunchtime, sometimes eating what was on our 'table' and sometimes from someone else's. He didn't think the other picnics were 'out of bounds' to him. None of my family were angry towards him for his actions. We all loved it. We were a family and its what families do! Oh if only the whole Church would operate this way in a region.

Every Christian has been adorned by the Spirit with gifts and talents to place on the 'table.' Every cell group or congregation in town has been given gifts and ministries to be used, not just in their own meetings, but in the building up of the whole expression of the Church in town, if needed. When one 'limb' in the Body of Christ is strong and has an abundance of certain gifts or ministries, yet another 'limb' is lacking in that area, then we must learn to share what we have for the common good. At the same time if you are the 'limb' that is lacking in any way, you must be humble enough to ask for help and then receive it. The goal must be for the whole Body of Christ to edify itself.

> *"from whom the whole body, joined and knit together by what every joint supplies, according to the effective working by which every part does its share, causes growth of the body for the edifying of itself in love." (Eph 4:16)*

Paul shows clearly the Body of Christ is strengthened, edified, grows and is brought into unity, when every joint, or part of the Body, supplies to the other. You cannot give what you didn't first receive. If you feely received it, then freely give it (Matt 10:8), for the common good and welfare of Christ in His Body. He gave it for you to contribute. When the Body of Christ operates, the way it primarily does, then we have a dis-connected, dis-jointed Body, which means we are drastically weakened in ability, to fulfill the task given us. Is this the way He desires us to operate? Is Christ divided? No, my friend, this model may be the Church's mode of operation, but is not Heaven's.

> *"And not only that, but we also rejoice in God through our Lord Jesus Christ, through whom we have now received the **reconciliation**." (Rom 5:11)*

> *"Now all things are of God, who has **reconciled** us to Himself through Jesus Christ, and has given us the **ministry of reconciliation**, that is, that God was in Christ reconciling the world to Himself, not imputing their trespasses to them, and has committed to us **the word of reconciliation**." (2Cor 5:18-19)*

Reconciliation is the fundamental ministry of Jesus. If it is the ministry of the 'Head,' then it is the ministry of the Body. There can be no argument to this. He has done the work for all to be reconciled. We, the Church, just reach out with that good news to all people everywhere. We are reconcilers. It is who we are, if the same Spirit that raised Him from the dead, dwells and lives in us (Rom 8:11).

"do this in remembrance of Me." (1Cor 11:24-25)

The Ministry of Re-Membering

The word 'remembrance' means to 'recall, bring back into memory, recollect, weigh well and consider.' The implication means we are to take this as a serious matter, to bring back what has been forgotten and what has been disconnected from us. The opposite of remembrance is dis-member. Yes, this word instantly clears up the fog and gets your attention. The Lord's Table, Lord's Supper, Breaking of Bread or Communion all point to one and the same message. It's a place of re-membering what has been dis-membered.

When you take the bread and cup, I am sure it reminds, brings back to the forefront of your thinking, that when you were yet a sinner Jesus died for you and forgave you your sin, His death becoming the bridge that reconciled you and the Father. Although it reminds you of the gruesome death He suffered on your behalf, surely there is also a place where you are thankful and grateful for Him doing it? He was innocent, yet for the Father's and your sake, He accepted the blame and guilt gladly, to see the reconciliation. Can we not find it in ourselves to love the Father the same way to bring reconciliation to the Body of Christ? There are no innocent ones on the earth;

"All have sinned and fallen short of the glory of God." (Rom 3:23)

Relationships in marriages, families, Church groups and people groups have all broken down purely because someone needed to blame someone for something and the other refused to accept the blame. It never seems to enter our thoughts that both parties could be wrong or right. We just seem to always believe we are the ones that are right. Being right and blaming the other seems more important than accepting the blame when you are innocent, to keep the relationship. The disciples had this same problem;

"Now as Jesus passed by, He saw a man who was blind from birth. And His disciples asked Him, saying, "Rabbi, who sinned, this man or his parents, that he was born blind?" Jesus answered, "Neither this man nor his parents sinned, but that the works of God should be revealed in him." (John 9:1-3)

The disciples needed to find out who to blame for the problem. After all, it must be someone's fault. Jesus didn't get drawn into the blame game. He showed, every situation that was out of alignment with God's blueprint, was an opportunity to reconcile it to bring glory to God. He healed the blind man.

So, if there is division in the Church in your region, then it is the opportunity to be reconciled in order to bring glory to God. Where there is a marriage or family breakdown, there is this same opportunity. In fact, this is what the Church should be known for in the world. But I ask, is it?

In Ruth Chapter four, we find the account of Boaz redeeming Ruth to become his wife. This legal transaction takes place in the city gate of Bethlehem. The gate of the city was the legal court room and it was here that the Elders gathered to discuss legal matters that effected the city and it's region. The Elders ruled on behalf of God and the people. Their decision was binding and God witnessed it. This is so important. If the natural Elders sat at the gates and ruled, then it is also essential we understand the natural points to the spiritual.

He who controls the spiritual gate of the city controls the spiritual condition of the city. But if the spiritual Elders do not gather in unity, then the city gate, which speaks of the 'portal' of the city, is not guarded and protected, but is open to the enemy. It is time the spiritual elders (the five-fold ministry team) of the city and region, were reconciled of their differences. This new day is calling them to gather together to praise, pray, prophesy and establish God's plan over the region. When they do, then God will honor their unity and bring the canopy of His presence over that region and the spiritual climate will change.

CHAPTER 11

The Multiplication

Opening The Doors For Business

When the **MESSENGER** and **MESSAGE** match the **MISSION**, to restore the **MESS** in the chosen **MULTITUDE**, using God's eternal **METHOD**, **MODEL** and **MOTIVATION**, delivered at the **MOMENT** of His prompting, it brings supernatural **MULTIPLICATION** and the realignment of all things, into His likeness.

DNA carries the attributes of the one it comes from. In the New Testament the 'seed' of the Father also refers to the first born son who inherits everything the father has. Jesus is the 'Seed' of the Father (Gen 3:15). The Seed holds the fullness of the Father (Col 1:19; 2:9). Every born again believer has received Christ, the Seed of the Father and of His fullness (John 1:16; Eph 1:23; 1Pet 1:23). The fullness of God that fills each believer increases in influence, when the whole Body of Christ stands in a place of agreement, working in a spirit of unity (Eph 1:23; 4:13).

Time To Open The Doors of The Treasury!

Everyone born of God, is made in the image and likeness of the Father. God is full of every good thing pertaining to life and godliness. God dwells in us (James 1:17; 2 Pet 1:1- 4). Therefore, every believer is full of the same precious and priceless deposits that dwell in God. All God is and has, is found in His 'sons' in seed form. Whatever His Kingdom is, dwells within every child of God. Whatever qualities Heaven has, they have already been deposited within the family of God, for we already have eternal life! We are the Treasury of God, the bank vault of God in earth, having received a down-payment of more to come;

> *"In Him you also trusted, after you heard the word of truth, the gospel of your salvation; in whom also, having believed, you were sealed (down-payment) with the Holy Spirit of promise,(of more to come)" (Eph 1:13).*

If you give away to others the gift He has deposited in you, He will see to it that His deposit matures and grows. What a great investment. Why would you keep it contained? It is time to invest what He has given you.

The role of leadership is not to control the Treasury of Heaven. That's God's job. The leader's job is to help every believer know and believe they are the Treasury of Heaven on earth and to help the believer open their doors for business!

Heaven has a currency and an exchange rate! The currency is the Promise note (the covenant), which is signed with His Name and in His own blood. The exchange rate is priceless for worthless. A robe of perfect righteousness in exchange for filthy garments of sin. He has exchanged sickness, disease, anxiety, fear and lack, with health, wholeness, peace, unconditional love and abundance. His death for your eternal life. The gifts and ministries within every believer, are the abilities of God for this exchange to be announced and activated in every person. The exchange is for all who hear, believe and receive it.

"Heaven has a currency and an exchange rate!"

The evidence of real leadership, is not revealed by charisma on a platform, but in willingness to release the deposit and gifts of God in every believer. When a Church is focused more upon releasing the leader's vision and gifting, rather than the congregations, then it may be flowing well, but they are not operating in the true gift of leadership.

A true father is not just concerned with having a home full of subservient children. The evidence of a true fathering spirit, is their ability to raise children into mature adults, who have the confidence to go out into this world and fulfill their dreams. A father 'sees' the hidden potential in every one of his children and helps the child to grow in it's awareness of it's gifting and will do everything they can, to help develop the child's gift and bring it to the surface. To the measure I do this, is the measure of my leadership ability and fruitfulness.

"I Can Do It!"

When Matt, my son, was just a toddler, we had an old type record player. Remember them? There was a long, slow and fiddly process to get it to play an LP. The whole event used to really fascinate Matt, who continually wanted the music to play. Increasingly, he wanted to help me load the LP and start the mechanism going. He would always cry out, "I can do it. I can do it." My response was to remind him he couldn't, due to his being so young. Daily there was a battle to keep him away from the record-player to prevent him ruining our LP's. But it was a futile battle and one I was destined to lose.

One morning, before dawn, the deafening sound of the Beatles blasting out "HELP, I need somebody," woke me and startled me into action. Almost falling down the stairs in a stupor, I saw Matt sitting there smiling and applauding himself, saying 'good boy, good boy!' I was not annoyed with him at all. I was stunned. He had proven to me he **did** have the ability to do what I thought he couldn't do. He had proven me wrong. A lesson I would experience many more times in the years ahead.

I decided that morning that if he showed any sort of desire to attempt to do a thing, then he must be ready to learn to do it properly. So instead of fighting his ability, I recognized and enabled it, helping him to do something correctly from the beginning. Oh yes, he made mistakes and there were some LP's so badly scratched they became unplayable, but the cost was worth it to see the creative ability within my son, regularly surface and shock me. There was more within him at such a tiny age, than I dreamed possible.

I discovered that day, that it wasn't that he did not have the ability, to do it, but that I did not have the ability to see just what he could do. It was my stinking thinking that was the problem, not his age or ability. He knew he could do it, that is why he battled with us so hard. He had a vision and a dream to do it and I, his father, was the hindering one, because I couldn't see what he could see. Oh how true is this in Church life everywhere.

Corks or Catalysts?

This lesson motivates me now as a leader in the kingdom of God, to know there are people sitting in churches everywhere, with a belief and a dream to do something great for God. Yet, they sit in churches with such a rigid system, that instead of leaders being the catalysts to people, they are instead, often corks in the bottle.

> *"Then God said, "Let the earth bring forth grass, the herb that yields seed, and the fruit tree that yields fruit according to its kind, whose seed is in itself, on the earth"; and it was so." (Gen 1:11)*

From the very first page of the Bible, we see God created all things with the ability to reproduce themselves. Reproduction is a basic 'law' of life. Fruit is the external evidence of an inward life. The supernatural life of God within you, is to be evidenced by the ministry gift, the gifts and the fruit of the Spirit externally, when grace makes me believe it possible.
Jesus said a tree was created to be fruitful (Luke 13:7-9), and if it wasn't, then uproot it and cast it aside. Why? Because it is not reflecting His nature, or fulfilling it's purpose and potential.
Dear reader, you are filled with the unlimited abilities and resources of God Himself. Do **not** let any man, women or system limit what God can do through you. Do not let your stinking thinking lock up the Treasury of God within you. Release the unlimited abilities of God.

Tens of thousands of the 'Treasury's' of God, attend church gatherings on Sunday mornings, which are led by the 'ministry team' made up of a few dozen people. Congregations are instructed when to stand, sing, sit, pray, shout, clap, give their offering and leave. The God-given gifts and abilities within thousands of people, almost never expressed, except through the praise time and the offering.
Weekly they go through this same ritual of church attendance, always receiving and taking, seemingly never brought to the place where they

can truly give back to Jesus what He gave to them. If we multiply this picture across every city and nation, the numbers are staggering. The majority of the royal priesthood is not ministering, but watching.

Imagine how effective we would be if we reversed this picture. The multiplication and growth would go off the charts. Miracles and ministries would be released in the community and discipleship groups would flourish across regions. Every section of life would be effected with ease. Leadership would be unable to control it, because it would be so diverse and happen so swiftly, as the Holy Spirit would initiate and enable it all. What joy it would bring in the family of God.

"The majority of the royal priesthood is not ministering, but watching."

Constantly the people of God are telling us they have become bored with 'Church.' They have lost their passion for meetings. Leaders and congregations feel the same. Leaders of large 'successful' Churches, have disclosed to Gwenda and I, that they are bored in the ministry. Yet, **they** have built the Church as they wanted it to be? It has achieved exactly what they dreamed of achieving. Yet, they are dissatisfied and bored with it all.

No-one is bored with Jesus. It is the system that has taken away their joy. Life reproduces life (Gen 10:1; Matt 1:1). Meetings and church structures don't.

The Church isn't meant to be built upon or around anyone, other than Jesus Christ. The goal of Church ministry for too long, has been to structure everything in such a way that it revolves around and elevates key leaders or ministries. If we used a pyramid to portray structure, then most leadership models would place leadership at the top and everything underneath. What Paul teaches us is the opposite to this picture (Eph 4:11-16). He likens leadership to those that prepare others to do the work of the ministry. We are just like the cooks and servers in an army canteen. Our role is prepare and serve the food, that strengthens and enables the ranks of soldiers to win the battle. Leaders need to be the foundations giving solid support for everyone else to do what God has called them to do. We lift and hold them up and everything points to Jesus at the top. He is the pinnacle. Though a King, He became the servant of all. He took the lower place and was elevated to the top. This is His model of leadership. Everything we do must point upwards to Jesus, to make Him the focus of the Church.

What Comes In, Must Swiftly Go Out!

Constipation happens when people consume food at one end of their body, but nothing flows out the other end! God in His wonderful wisdom and mercy, gave us a hole at the top and the bottom of our body. If the outlet is not working in co-ordination with the inlet, then the digested food sits in the persons bowels releasing toxic poisoning. Toxic poison will then enter the blood stream, slowly effecting every part of their being. The person loses their strength, balance, vision and ability to comprehend. They are slowly dying, all because they are taking in but not giving out.

The natural teaches us the spiritual truth. People will spiritually stagnate and lose their vision, joy, strength, enthusiasm and become disillusioned, if all they do is keep taking in, but never get the proper chance to give out what they have received.

"Freely you have received, freely give." (Matt 10:8)

Is this all because of poor leadership? Absolutely not. I repeat myself. No-one needs anyone's permission to do what God told them to do. You have His permission. You may need the help of leaders to prepare you and help achieve the best results, but it is clearly the responsibility of every believer to just do what God told them to do. In the end you will not be accountable to your Church leader for doing or not doing

God's will. You will be personally accountable to God Himself, for what you did with what He gave you.

"No-one needs anyone's permission to do what God told them to do. "

I know the common teaching for years has declared that the leader is responsible to God for your soul. But they are not. They cannot be. This takes away all responsibility of my life away from me and gives it to another person. I am responsible for my life, no-one else. A leader is responsible for who they are towards you, not for you. They are responsible before God, to give the best leadership they can give, with the greatest wisdom and teaching they can possibly give to you.

"I have come that they may have life, and that they may have it more abundantly." (John 10:10)

The Priesthood Of All Believers

Billy Graham apparently once said, that if he continued to hold crusades every day of the week, for the rest of his life and lead a thousand people to Christ in each meeting, then the Church would think he was very successful. Yet, at the end, he would have reached a fraction of the earth's population (presently over seven billion people). He then suggested a new model. He showed that if he led one person to the Lord, spent a whole year discipling them, then both he and this new believer repeated the process the following year, in 24 months he would have just himself and three converts to Christ and the Church would think he had failed.

But if those same four people repeated the process the next year, and continued to follow this same format year upon year, then mathematically the whole world could be reached and saved in one generation. My friend, let this principle soak into your imagination a moment. What everyone has been waiting for is within our grasp, if we adopt Heaven's blueprint.

Billy Graham's analogy was questioning why we continue to do Church the way we do, when it isn't effective and as fruitful as it could be, if we used the method of true discipleship, that Jesus and the New Testament Church used.

> *"praising God and having favor with all the people. And the Lord added to the church daily those who were being saved."* (Acts 2:47)

> *"Then the word of God spread, and the number of the disciples multiplied greatly in Jerusalem, and a great many of the priests were obedient to the faith."* (Acts 6:7)

At the birth of the Church the Lord 'added' to the Church. But as the Church continued something changed. Instead of being able to 'add' they entered the realm of multiplication. The believers went from leading one to the Lord, to leading many at the same time. The speed increased.

People were born again into the early Church with the full understanding that they would be discipled in order to reproduce what they had learnt, in others. They lived with the whole understanding that their life was to be lived to extend the kingdom of God into all of their world. Leaders equipped them with the principles and disciplines necessary, to ensure the rapid expansion of His kingdom in the hearts of people everywhere. They were mission focused, not meetings orientated. When its all down to the pastor, or the system, then any growth is limited by the ability of that one person and system. But when it is reproduced into every believer, not constrained by a limiting structure, then it can become an exponential explosion of life, as the Spirit moves freely through all.

New Testament Leadership Model For Correct Alignment!

I believe the New Testament shows that todays normal Church leadership style is often out of alignment with the New Testament model and therefore causes much of Church life to also be out of alignment with the Word of God. Again I say, this is not an accusation, but based upon my personal experience of almost 40 years of studying the Word and being involved in ministry leadership.

I injured my ankle a few years ago. It was painful and unable to take the full load of the weight of my body. I automatically compensated for it, by altering the way I walked. Slowly I started having pain in my knee, followed by my hips, back and shoulders. The damage in my ankle had caused the rest of my body to move out of alignment to compensate and it was causing me pain. The one thing that was wrong was causing other problems in my body. Thankfully, my ankle healed and I experienced my whole body slowly readjust and realign itself. It taught me a deep spiritual lesson about correct alignment in the Body of Christ!

New Testament leadership consisted of only two offices. Elders and Deacons. Neither are referred to as titles. They are mentioned using the plural version of the word, except when the writer writes of an individual. Their leadership model was not one individual in charge doing everything, but a plurality of leadership making sure everything is done in order and with balance.

The 'five-fold' ministry names, were not positions, offices or titles. They were functions. Paul, Peter, James and Jude, all write letters beginning with their names followed by 'an apostle,' or 'a bond servant of Jesus Christ.' Never as a title. People love titles and the places of importance. They love the praises of men rather than the praise of Jesus (John 12:43). Being called 'son' by God the Father, is greater to me than being called Archbishop, Apostle, Psalmist and Teacher Goss by man. Why would I want an inferior title?

The New Testament Church was not hierarchal in any way. The five-fold ministry names are simply functions some are called to do.

In the Old Testament you had the two offices of Priests and Levites. In the New Testament it is Elders and Deacons. The elder's role was to take care and oversight of the 'spiritual' aspects of the people, whilst the deacons oversaw the more practical aspects. But both functions are spiritual. Both are manifestations of God's grace and anointing. Is being a husband and father more important or spiritual than being a wife and mother? It is not about positions, authority or being more important than another. It is purely functional issues. Some are gifted to communicate, some to oversee kitchens and food distribution. Some are musical and dramatic orientated, whilst others have a grace upon them to lead people to Christ. All gifts are the manifestation of the one Spirit of God. One part of God is not better than another. Nor is one part of the Body of Christ more important than another. All are equally important.

> *"Then I was given a reed like a measuring rod. And the angel stood, saying, "Rise and **measure** the temple of God, the altar, and those who worship there." (Rev 11:1)*

The issue of measuring runs from the Book of Exodus to Revelation showing the Lord is extremely concerned with what is being built for Him. He has a blueprint, which we discussed in earlier chapters. His blueprint is Christ. Everything we are and do is measured and compared to the 'original' or authentic one. Notice, it is John, an apostle, who is given the measuring reed. This doesn't make the apostle any more important than anyone else. But they do have a serious function in the Church today, as much as they did two thousand years ago.

God has gifted them with the ability and grace to get done the job of aligning or realigning the Church, to His heavenly pattern. He has also given them His authority to see it gets done. It is up to us to recognize and receive them as sent of God, for them to accomplish their task.

Fathers Of The Faith

The apostles raised up the eldership over the city and nation (Titus 1:5). The apostles vision is to raise up people, not buildings. They discover, by the Spirit, those graced of God to be the elders and leaders of a region. They train and ordain them before the people. The elder did not work isolated from the other elders in that region. The apostle brings the complete understanding of team ministry. Team ministry brings accountability and balance to the Church, like the husband and wife, mother and father bring to a home.

The word 'elder' is not referring to natural age, but maturity of their walk with God. Eldership was not the second tier of leadership under the pastor, as it seems today. The elders **were** the leaders.
The five-fold minister is part of the eldership team God is raising up in a region, to build His house. They are like the pillars in the house, that provide the stability and strength, to hold everything in place. They are the ones raised of God, who have a proven character of balance and a thorough knowledge and grasp of the Word of God. Their character of leadership has been revealed by their home life and family atmosphere. If they cannot raise their family in alignment with the Kingdom of God and God's purposes, then how will they do it in the larger and wider family of God? These are not new converts or a novices in the things of God (1Tim 3:1-7). They are the ones forged and molded by God through the fires of adversity and proven faithful.

The early Church elders were known as 'fathers of the faith.' Spiritual fathers reproduce who Jesus is, in the 'sons' of God (1 Cor 11:1). They didn't fashion people after themselves. They pointed to the greater and perfect blueprint, the Son of God. Paul said;

"Imitate me, just as I also imitate (mimic) Christ." (1Cor 11:1)

They pointed upwards, continually lifting people's vision onto Christ. They raised people with the ability to look on Him, the founder and finisher of their faith. They did not build everything around themselves, their ministry, or their 'vision.' True fathers of the faith have only one desire. To build everyone and everything in alignment to Him and to enable every believer to know, hear and obey God for themselves and to teach others to do the same. They have a vision for multiplying, not adding to the Church. The early Church rapidly multiplied, filling the nations with disciples of Christ, who readily laid down their lives for His gospel. The general public were in awe of this entity called 'The Way' (Acts 5:11). Books were written by secular authors, who spoke reverently about the love the people of 'The Way' had for Jesus and the Godly attitudes and traits of the Church community. Everyone knew of their presence, and His presence within them. I wonder if we, the Church of today, suddenly vanished into Heaven, would anyone notice? Would anyone grieve at the loss of the Church from their community?

Together, the eldership oversaw the work and mission of the church. They 'oversaw.' They didn't control and organize everything, telling everyone what to do all the time. They were mature and confident that the Holy Spirit is the very best teacher of all. He would be with the people at all times to guide them, when the leaders weren't.
They would be just there to share the wisdom imparted to them, from God, into the believers.
(A more detailed study on this subject is found in my AFA Leadership Manual)

If I had the choice to live fully in the power of the life of His Spirit, effecting this world the way He did, which included the consequence of persecution, or a life that is based in meetings, which ultimately produce in me a life of disillusionment, complacency and unfruitfulness, then, I can firmly and confidently say I would take the first option. Will you?

My friend, I urge you, be loyal to the new 'Man' (Jesus), His Moment, Message, Mission, Motivation and Method of Multiplying Himself in the earth and you will truly see evidence of His Kingdom effecting the Mess of this world. It may not always be a comfortable road to travel, but it will bear fruit and fruit evidences real disciples and followers of Christ.

CHAPTER 12

The Multitude

"That The House May Be Filled"

When the **MESSENGER** and **MESSAGE** match the **MISSION**, to restore the **MESS** in the chosen **MULTITUDE**, using God's eternal **METHOD**, **MODEL** and **MOTIVATION**, delivered at the **MOMENT** of His prompting, it brings supernatural **MULTIPLICATION** and the realignment of all things, into His likeness.

"So that servant came and reported these things to the Master. Then the Master of the house, being angry, said to his servant, 'Go out quickly into the streets and lanes of the city, and bring in here the poor, and the maimed, the lame and the blind. ...... Then the Master said to the servant, 'Go out into the highways and hedges, and compel them to come in, that my house may be filled." (Lk 14:21-23)

Fill His House!

Embedded in this parable is a truth that if applied, I believe will turn normal Church practices on its head. The Master mentioned is Jesus. The servants are His messengers who go out with the urgent message and invitation to attend the supper. The first group that received the invitation used excuses of why they couldn't attend.

Who were these people rejecting the invitation? Well, if you look back to the beginning of Luke Chapter 14, you will discover that Jesus is in a Pharisee's house having a meal with the religious and legal leaders. He is using the parable when speaking to them. So I believe He is saying it to the legalistic people within the religious system. He was offering a new way for them to live, with a new vision of how to fulfill His commission. Being rejected, the offer is therefore given to the lowly and poor, who responded and came. But still there was room, so the Master threw out the invitation even further. He was determined to have a full house. The offer went out to all.

There is a truth, revealed in this passage, so subtle it can easily be overlooked. He wants His house, not Temple filled. For too long the emphasis of Church life has been to go out and bring the lost into the Church. But it doesn't say anywhere, in the New Testament, to bring people into the Church system. In fact, it repeatedly tells us and shows us, we are called to go out to the people, not bring them in our Church meetings.

In this passage it shows a biblical truth that is revealed constantly in the New Testament, which has been so overlooked. The emphasis is to bring people into His 'House.'

Jesus is sitting in a house, instructing the spiritual leaders of the day who are holding fast to that old worn out system of the day, as so many do today. He is wanting to completely change its concept, emphasis and mode of operation (as He is today), from looking to fill a Temple, to looking to fill a house. The passage says Jesus told them 'bring in here.' Bring in where? He was not in the Temple, but a family home. The emphasis is "House before Temple." May I humbly suggest the Church has been doing it backwards for so long? We put the emphasis upon meetings in the Church building, not upon releasing the presence and power of God from within the person's home. The focus is drawing people out of their place and sphere of influence to operate in a central location, when it needs to be vice versa.

This emphasis and order was revealed to King David when desiring to bring the Ark (God's presence and governmental authority) from the lowlands of Kirath-Jearim up to the highland mountain top of Zion, the center of Jerusalem (see 2Sam 6:1-12).

David's chosen method of transporting the Ark of God, was to use a brand new cart driven by a pair of oxen. But this was not the prescribed way as shown to Moses. God told Moses the Ark must be covered over and carried on two poles on the shoulders of the Levites (Ex 25:13-15; Num 4:1,15-16). God is a God of order (1Cor 14:40). David didn't adhere to God's way. Instead he chose to use a man-made cart driven by oxen. He did not understand you cannot drive the presence of God, you can only carry it. It is to be upon our shoulders. His presence rests within us, His priesthood of all believers (1Pet 2:9). Man-made ideas and strategies may excite, but will not work. They may entertain people and even fill an auditorium. But they will not change the spiritual climate of a region or generation. Only God's presence and governmental power will do that when we operate and are in alignment with His blueprint. And we have been given by Him, the instructions on how to bring His presence, power and authority to bear influence in a community and nation.

To David and the people of Israel, everything is looking good and going well, just like so much of Church life today! Everyone is celebrating and moving forward. What could possibly be wrong? Suddenly, there is an abrupt halt to their celebrations as their man-made invention tilts as the oxen stumble. The Ark begins to slide across the cart, everyone guessing the Ark will topple and crash to the floor. Instinctively, a young priest presumptuously put out a hand to prop up God (the Ark) and stop it falling. At that very moment the power of God unseen in 120 years, suddenly breaks loose and kills this young man. The celebration was over in a moment. Silence hit the scene. All eyes were upon the leader. He had no answers for why his scheme had been brought to such a sudden and calamitous end.

A young man called Obed-Edom, stood on the corner of the street and had seen this devastating moment. He was called on by David, to take the Ark into his home, to look after it until they worked out why the Lord had allowed this to happen.

I can picture the shock and horror on Obed-Edom's face when the King says this to him. He loves and honors his King and would never desire to disobey or disrespect him in any way. But he would not want to place it in his front room, when what happened to Uzzah may happen to him. Would you?

If I was faced with this dilemma, I think I would try to persuade the King that my house wasn't glorious or regal enough for such an honor to be given to me and suggest one of my neighbors houses was much more prestigious for such a task. Never-the-less, the Ark enters the home of Obed-Edom.

This is a moment of real confusion for David and Israel, and a day of fear for Obed-Edom and his family. This sudden, unexpected event has everyone praying. David for wisdom and Obed-Edom for protection and mercy. But the plan that had gone completely wrong, was about to unveil God's plan and way to bring His presence back into the nations. Within weeks, Obed-Edom is prospering so much at home and work, that the news of his miraculous prosperity finds it's way to the Kings palace in Zion. It encourages David that God is not angry with him, or the nation.

The Ark's presence literally pulled Obed-Edom into alignment with the attributes of itself. Obed-Edom didn't make it happen. Gods presence and power did. It was the grace of God at work, because He was received and remained in the center of a home. Obed-Edom simply received from God. The honor and favor on God simply came on Obed-Edom and on all he had and did. God hasn't changed. What He did for Obed-Edom, He is wanting to do for us.

Our History Never Determines Our Future

Obed-Edom is a Gittite, one of Goliath's descendants. David had killed Goliath as a young boy some years beforehand. He also killed all of Goliath's family. I am sure the defeat for that tribe left them devastated, with a sense of shame upon everyone. They became the slaves of Israel.

"Our history does not determine our future."

Thank God our history does not determine our future. The Ark of God was passing this house of Obed-Edom and decided that this was the moment to break the chains of slavery, poverty and shame from this young mans household. When the Ark of God entered Obed-Edom's house, the blessing on God broke the curse on Obed-Edom's family, and it will today for you, your household and your community. Make no mistake, God is not surprised by who gets born into His Kingdom. It was He that organized every detail and event in and around your life that brought you to the place to accept His invitation into His house. And the moment you entered, every curse was broken my friend. The presence and governmental power of God will continue to pour out His blessings into your life, until it is evident to everyone, that the curses once upon your life, have been removed from you once and for all.

David and his team, searched the scriptures and discovered where they got it so badly wrong. They discovered two things. They hadn't prepared a place for God's presence (1Chron 15:1) and God's method of transport for bringing the Ark into the city was not on a nice man-made structure (cart), but carried upon the shoulders of the Levites. (Ex 27:7; 1Chron 15:2). It's not a system that carries God's presence and anointing, but people whose hearts are towards Him. We MUST see this principle in order to see the dormant power of God released once again, into our communities and nations. Our focus must be upon people, who are the House of God, not upon a physical building we love to call 'The House of God,' which it obviously isn't.

David and his leaders repented of their arrogance before God and brought their plan into alignment with God's. Once again, we see the issue of the Spirit revealing where something is out of alignment with God's blueprint, through a painful experience. It is followed by the account how everything changes the moment realignment happens.

David calls everyone to come to meet him at Obed-Edom's house, to bring up the Ark of the Lord to it's resting place in Zion. They obtain a different response from Obed-Edom to the last time they were outside his front door. This time he begs David not to remove the Ark from his home. Three months earlier he had been pleading to not receive the Ark. Now he is pleading for it not to be removed. There must have been some sort of negotiating going on between Obed-Edom and the King, because in 1Chron 15:24, you find Obed-Edom has become a doorkeeper for the Ark on Zion. He must have determined that if David would not let him keep the Ark in his home, then he was moving his home to be near the Ark. He was not willing to let go of the presence of God, because he has come to know how everything is turned around in a moment by His presence and grace.

Obed-Edom becomes the doorkeeper of the Ark. The Ark is the presence of God's Treasury. 'Doors' speak of the 'portals' of God, mentioned in earlier chapters. The worshipper and lover of God's presence, is the doorkeeper of God's Treasury.

I want you to see another gem of truth 'hidden' in this whole account. David and the people tried to take the Ark of God's presence into the City of David. It stalled and stopped and had to be placed inside a home. Finally, the account ends with them coming back for it 3 months later and carrying it to Zion. Did you 'see' it? The truth and strategy hidden in this passage is that the Ark had to go via the home before it took its rightful place in the city. It did not go into the city and end up in the home. It was vice versa.

Re-covering The Nation With Worship

I have tried throughout this whole book to show God has a pattern for us to build by, that will bring us all the blessings of God that we are looking for. The pattern of God, so clearly shown here is that a place for His presence is to be prepared in the home first, then the city. Congregational Church life is meant to be the overflow of all God is doing in my home, not the other way around. Daily I can see the presence and power of God operating in and through my home. I don't have to wait to attend a service one day a week in a building somewhere in town, in order to get 'topped up' so I can survive another week in the world. God's way is for me to enjoy His presence and power all day, every day at home or in work. Then when we gather together we explode with joy and praise because we have been filled up with Him daily and our gatherings become the venue of the overflow, not the source.

> *"Go out quickly into the **streets and lanes** of the city, and **bring in here**......"* (Lk 14:21) (emphasis mine)

Jesus' command to the servant (us), was to go out into the streets and lanes of the city. Jesus' invitation was to invite people "in here." He was in a house when stating this. Something impacted me one day and showed me the way to reach a community with His **Message**. It is by using His **Method**! Sounds simple right? Then why don't we try using it?

In 1979 I returned from the Bible College of Wales to my home town Bridgend. My wife Anne and I had sold our home to attend the college and on our return stayed with my parents until the Lord opened the door for us to find a new place to live. My experience in Bible College had transformed my life completely and I rose very early every morning to worship and read the Word.

It was on one of these mornings that I sensed the Lord burdening me to pray for my own nation of Wales. I began to pray for revival fire to be ignited, like bonfires, in every street and town across the land. I must have shared this burden with someone I knew, because within a few days I was using my parent's living room to hold a worship and prayer gathering, once a week. A small group of people had joined with me in this endeavor to cover Wales with small groups of people who would pray at specific times of each day until the nation was covered with homes worshipping over Wales twenty-four hours a day, seven days a week.

After a few weeks I received a message that a family in a town, not far from Bridgend, wanted to do the same and asked permission to join our prayer network and strategy. "Join our strategy and network?" We had no network or real strategy. All we had, I thought, was a commission and burden from the Lord to do what we were doing. We had no understanding of what was about to be birthed. Our obedience to the Holy Spirit's prompting had sparked an inspiration, in another town locally, to do the same thing. Over the next few months we received phone-calls and letters, from all over Wales, requesting to be linked in to this divine network, totally unorganized, that was simply organically evolving before us. Wales was being re-covered with worship cells.

The South Wales Revival Crusade

It was during this time I was surprisingly and suddenly pushed into holding a public evangelistic ministry. We called it The South Wales Revival Crusade and held meetings in local halls and Church buildings.

Hundreds came to Christ followed by many many healing's, miracles and deliverances. Empty Church buildings began to overflow with people in just a few weeks or months.

At the same time my family and I moved into a new home in a street we knew nothing about. We desperately needed a home of our own to live in and we had been praying for the Lord to grant us a miracle home. Within three weeks He had done it for us and we moved in.

I fervently wanted to share the gospel with everyone, so I was praying for the Lord to show me how to do it, with people in this new street. Suddenly the Lord shared with me that He did not want me to go knocking on doors or do anything evangelistic. He just asked me to worship every day. Even when out walking, I sensed just to worship him as I walked my street. Then I began to sing prophetically over each and every home that I walked passed.

I can remember being really frustrated, because the more I worshipped over the street, the more a burden grew in my heart to see people saved and touched by His power. I wanted to tell people about Jesus. Once again He spoke clearly and said, "I don't want you to show me what you can do for Me. I want to show you what I can do for you." It puzzled me. But I knew deeply that the Lord was doing something in my life that would transform the way I thought about the ministry.

Just a couple of months later, on a day of torrential rain, my wife asked me to go to the local supermarket to get her something she needed for our evening meal. I started to drive up the street, the rain so heavy that windscreen wipers were hardly helping me. I was moving very slowly.

As I got to the end of the street, I saw a lady standing outside her home, battling to hold on to her umbrella in the wind and rain. I heard the voice of the Holy Spirit within me quietly tell me to stop and give her a ride. I didn't want to stop because I was short of time. So I tried to ignore His request. This happened again and my response was an even stronger 'No!" A third time He repeated His request. Before I could open my mouth to respond, something miraculous and strange occurred. Immediately someone put the brakes on my car and turned the ignition off and I unintentionally stopped immediately, right in front of this lady called Dorothy.

I was looking down at my feet still wondering what had happened, when she, thinking I had stopped to offer her a ride, opened the door, jumped in as fast as she could, and gratefully thanked me for being so kind! I was dumbstruck. She was in my car and kept thanking me and saying it was so kind of me to help her a total stranger in this way. At that moment I felt ashamed, because I knew the truth, but the Holy Spirit had made me look great in her eyes.

Dorothy was going to the same supermarket, so I offered to wait for her and give her a ride back home. Somewhere on this five minute journey, she turned to me and said "Your a preacher aren't you?" I was completely shocked. How could she know this as we had never met and I had only moved into her street a few months earlier. I confirmed I was and hastily asked her how she knew this. "Oh", she replied, "everyone in the street knows who you are." I wondered how this could be? I had done no more than say a 'hello,' or 'good morning,' to individuals when I went out to walk up and down my street. She went on to explain everyone could hear me singing and praying every day because my bedroom window was always open.

I was speechless. The whole street knew who I was without me intentionally doing or saying anything to anyone!

Dorothy asked if I ever preached locally. I told her of the evangelistic meetings I held around the area and she quickly asked if she could attend the next one. Amazed, I told her that we were having one that very evening and I arranged to pick her up to take her to the meeting with us. It turned out that she also brought her daughter with her and both wonderfully received Jesus as their Lord and Savior that evening. I could hardly believe it. I had done nothing. Yet He had opened the door, quite supernaturally and now two new believers had entered His House.

Within a few days, Dorothy's daughter whom had received Christ as her Savior, was turning 18 years old, but had few friends. So we offered to invite friends from the Church to come the following

Sunday afternoon and have a little celebration for her birthday. About 20 people came to the party with us, bringing loads of food. Dorothy had invited her friend from the street to also come. All afternoon we had fun time telling funny stories and jokes. It was a great atmosphere. As we were all cleaning up after the event, I remember the lady from the street suddenly saying, "You can't be Christians because you laugh." I thought she was joking, but she was serious! It seemed no one in her Church ever laughed. Rather than criticize her Church and denomination, I simply told her my testimony of being filled with gratefulness to Jesus because He had rescued me on the very edge of committing suicide. Within minutes she softened and asked if she could come to one of our meetings. We didn't have one planned for weeks and not wishing to miss this open opportunity, I invited her instead, to a large evangelistic event that was taking place that coming Wednesday evening. She came and promptly gave her life to Jesus. In one week I had 3 new believers!

I decide I had better teach them the basics of this new life in Christ. We arranged to meet in this new lady's home. We were knocking on her door, the next morning, when a neighbor suddenly opened her door asking why we were all going into her neighbors house? Before I could respond, Dorothy told her everything and invited her to join us. She gladly responded, asking if her friend across the street could come as well. Dorothy shouted, "the more the merrier." so instead of three new believers in this room, we now had five people. Within an hour both of these new ladies had also turned their lives over to Jesus. This happened continually week after week until 32 people came into the Kingdom of God in a six week period.

We decided to open our home up to hold an evening meeting, so that we could teach the people who couldn't attend the morning coffee morning. The numbers kept growing, until over 40 people were attending, some driving 100 miles to attend. We literally watched Jesus' presence come into a whole street and effect the lives and futures of so many people, in such a short period of time, all without my help. My home had become the portal of Heaven. My times of worship had brought **Alignment For Assignment** into reality in my life and I was discovering that I was "**A Doorkeeper of the Treasury of God**!"

Back To My Roots!

Many years have passed since those early days of 1979/80. I have planted and led Churches, Bible Schools, Worships Schools and held many conferences across the nations.

In 2002 I was compelled by the Holy Spirit to '*Let go of everything you have ever known, to lay hold of everything you have ever dreamed of.*' (I tell of this account in my first book 'Don't Kick The Donkey- Ride it!') I have to admit, I had no real idea what that fully meant. But I think I do now. In 2002 I stepped down from all my focus and responsibilities in ministry in Wales. I knew I was beginning a new journey, that would prepare me for the years ahead when I knew I would once again see my focus restored to Wales. Over the fourteen years, since 2002, we have ministered in thousands of Church meetings, preparing the Church for the greatest move of God ever seen in our entire history, which I truly believe we stand on the verge of experiencing.

In January 2015, whilst in New Orleans, USA, I sensed the Holy Spirit was informing me that I was going back to my roots to fulfill the second part of the prophetic word He had given me in 1981. It was time to refocus on Wales.

Suddenly, invitations to preach in Wales came to us. They were in places where I first began to share my faith. Suddenly people I have not seen in over 30 years appeared in those meetings or reconnected with me. I was invited to preach in New Mill Full Gospel Church, Cardigan, the first place the Lord used me to lay hands upon the sick and see my first miracle take place. It was happening.

When the Lord said for me to 'return to your roots,' I thought He meant Wales, but He meant more than that. He meant to return me to recovering Wales with worship cells once again, with worship twenty-four hours a day, seven days a week. Back in 1979/80 we had a passion to see Wales restored to Him and for the nation to be filled with worshippers. We had no real strategy or network then. But we do now!

The fourteen years away from Wales, have embedded in us, the vision, the strategy and the blueprint of what will turn nations back to God and fulfill His commission. It is no longer 'South Wales Revival Crusade.' Now it is a world reaching focus on fulfilling His commission on making disciples of all nations. It is called '*in*HOPE' (*international network* of **H**ouses **O**f **P**raise and Evangelism). We are called to raise up 1 Million Houses of HOPE across the nations.

Will you help us? Will you turn your home into a Home Of Hope and recover Wales and the nations with worship of the Father? If you will, then join us and learn to turn your home and life into the portal of Heaven.

CHAPTER 13

The Vision of *in*HOPE

(*international* *network* of Houses Of Praise & Evangelism)

"Making Worship the Lifestyle of All Believers"

When the **MESSENGER** and **MESSAGE** match the **MISSION**, to restore the **MESS** in the chosen **MULTITUDE**, using God's eternal **METHOD, MODEL** and **MOTIVATION**, delivered at the **MOMENT** of His prompting, it brings supernatural **MULTIPLICATION** and the realignment of all things, into His likeness.

The vision of *in*HOPE was birthed in our spirits in the summer of 2006 when walking across the concourse of Houston Airport in Texas. I heard the Holy Spirit say, "raise up for me an international network of 1 Million Houses of H.O.P.E and teach them to change the spiritual climate in their areas through worship." As I heard His voice, I also saw a vision of houses suddenly flooded with light and the light jumped from house to house, street to street, until a nation was covered in a network of little lights. I was literally seeing the world slowly engulfed with the light of God's presence, like something out of control. It spread every direction, by the gusts of the wind (the Holy Spirit). It was breathtaking in it's impact, ability and swiftness at eradicating darkness from the globe.

I was stunned at the enormity of the task. But I knew, that if the Church had the courage to consider changing it's course (Mission) and mode of operations (Method) and instead of doing everything organizationally, built instead organically, moving where God is moving, then I was convinced the vision would flourish!

Our hearts were filled with God's purpose for the rest of our days. We knew we may never accomplish everything that was in our hearts, but we made the decision that day, to live and die, trying too. Our challenge was to ignite just one heart with the vision and equip them to disciple one more person with the same lifestyle and vision. We knew if each person repeated the process, then we could see something self perpetuating, unleashed and overseen by the Spirit of God, that would raise a generation of discipled worshippers of Jesus!!

Worshippers & Warriors

Our passion is to ignite every believer's heart, to know that they stand in Christ's full authority and that when everyone of us, fully grasp that we are the spiritual 'portals' of God for our communities, then we will make our homes a worshipping center in our community. A place where God's Spirit will reorder the spiritual climate.

My friend, we are in a spiritual war for the souls of billions of people on this planet. We cannot just pray in our prayer towers, we must also go down to the valley and confront our Goliath to break his control and influence over the nations. We must raise a generation of worshippers and warriors. We must raise a generation of believers who touch Heaven and change earth. A generation of Jacobs, aware of two worlds. Of Joseph's, who have a God given dream and no matter the battle and the rejection from those we dearly love around us, continue to hold fast to that dream and vision, knowing that in due season it shall come to pass (Habb 2:3).

CONNECT WITH US

Join us on this adventure, become a Home of H.O.P.E today
and see the vision come to pass:

www.wynnegoss.com

Join Wynne & Gwenda
For up to date information on our work, itinerary & resources,
or to sign up to receive our emails, please go to:

www.wynnegoss.com

Join Wynne on Facebook:

@wynne.goss